THE FELLOWSHIP OF HIS PRESENCE

The Reality of God Among Us

Keith Carroll

Newburg, Pennsylvania

The Fellowship of His Presence
by Keith Carroll
Copyright ©2018 Keith Carroll

All rights reserved. This book is protected under the copyright laws of the United States of America. This book may not be copied or reprinted for commercial gain or profit.

Unless otherwise identified, Scripture is taken from the *New American Standard Bible*, Copyright ©1960, 1962, 1963, 1968, 1971, 1973, 1975, 1977 by The Lockman Foundation.

Scripture marked KJV is taken from the King James Version of the Bible.

ISBN 978-0-9860923-5-0
For Worldwide Distribution
Printed in the U.S.A.

                     Relate2God Press
                       PO Box 341
                   Newburg, PA 17240

Contents

Introduction   *v*

1. Our Ever-Present Father   *1*
2. Our Growing Insights   *16*
3. True Light of Our Life   *35*
4. Learn From Ancient Experiences   *52*
5. Our Living Example   *71*
6. The Spirit of Truth Reveals   *88*
7. A Thirst for His Presence   *109*
8. Our Enlightening Guide   *125*
9. Today's Reigning King   *148*
10. Our Developing Reality   *168*

Special Thanks

For the inspiring fellowship
and contributions of my wife, Nancy;
Thelma and Gary Diehl;
Delores Ocker;
and Alice and Rocky Rockwell

For the invaluable editorial skills of
Brian and Kathy Banashak

And to Sam and Joan Eaton,
and Glen Reed
for their deeply rewarding fellowship

Introduction

A few years ago a close friend, who is the pastor of a well-established home church, asked me to consider giving a presentation on my understanding of the second coming of Christ to his fellowship. He is a pastor who encourages his group to closely examine doctrines or teachings as a means of clarifying what they believe to be true.

My friend said they had recently examined the two most common teachings on the second coming of Christ, and he felt it would be good to consider another approach. Over many breakfast conversations through the years, he learned that I viewed the scriptural teaching of the coming of Christ a bit differently than some.

Following a few days of prayerful consideration, I began organizing my thoughts and scriptural references for a presentation. As I worked on the content, I realized a verbal presentation would not allow enough time to do the concept justice. So I decided to write the message as a paper. With the addition of some fresh insights, the paper has now morphed into this book.

Dear reader, I ask you to consider my entire presentation before comparing it to another or defending your current understanding. Give it some time to get a feel for its validity. You'll find many familiar truths in this book and some that may challenge your assumptions. See if these fresh and new perceptions make sense to you, if you feel an inner witness—or not. Fair enough?

May your life be enriched as you read these pages!

God is

In us as a source of life

With us as our guide through this life

In our midst as a motivation for caring fellowship

Among us as a presence that helps our maturing process

Chapter 1

Our Ever-Present Father

You would probably find my teenage years rather unusual. My parents and I traveled extensively, visiting many ministries in our quest to understand who God is and how we should relate to Him. One particular location we visited set the stage for a unique insight into the nature of God.

Inside one of the buildings was a large room that contained a single painted mural, which spanned all four walls from ceiling to floor. An impressive presentation, the mural showed a variety of detailed scenes depicting human civilization: a large city with skyscrapers, smaller cities, rural towns, a few farms, plus a variety of jungle and desert areas along with villages.

Every area illustrated the interaction of people from modern cities to native habitats. Multiple modes of transportation depicted travel from one area to another. Everything was impressively connected as the mural ingeniously flowed from one area and activity to another.

Mesmerized, and as if drawn into the mural, I moved deliberately around the room, carefully examining each scene. Everything was beautifully connected, with each area displaying amazing detail. Finally I stood in the middle of the room to get a better feel for the overall presentation.

As I slowly turned around to observe the wonder of the full exhibit, I began to sense God saying to me, "This is a helpful visual of how I view everything in the natural realm. I am able to see it all at once without turning around. I observe all activity and even the movements of time simultaneously. This is how I know the end from the beginning."

My understanding of God's majesty greatly increased in that moment as I experienced a fresh glimpse of His awesome nature. The mural became a metaphor to me of God's omniscience and eternal nature. Have you ever had a similar experience yourself?

When we learn to view life as God sees it, everything fits together and makes sense. Like the mural, I hope to present understandable insight into God's design and purpose for our lives, as relational expressions of His vast nature. While I don't claim that my efforts are perfect, they are comprehensive.

A Big God

We learn through Scripture that God created the natural realm consisting of time, space, and matter. Since God created the material universe, we can conclude that He dwells beyond it. When we realize He exists beyond this natural realm, it is easier to understand that His essence is much greater than any physical reality.

The Bible describes God as a Spirit Being with very specific qualities. He is:

1) **Eternal**—having no beginning or end

> *Now to the King eternal, immortal, invisible, the only God, be honor and glory forever and ever. Amen* (1 Timothy 1:17).

> *Who alone possesses immortality and dwells in unapproachable light, whom no man has seen or can see. To Him be honor and eternal dominion!* (1 Timothy 6:16)

2) **Omnipresent**—simultaneously everywhere

> *Where can I go from Your Spirit? Or where can I flee from Your presence?* (Psalm 139:7)

3) **Omnipotent**—all-powerful

> *Can you discover the depths of God? Can you discover the limits of the Almighty?* (Job 11:7)

> *Ah Lord GOD! Behold, You have made the heavens and the earth by Your great power and by Your outstretched arm! Nothing is too difficult for You* (Jeremiah 32:17).

4) **Omniscient**—all knowing

> *O LORD, You have searched me and known me. You know when I sit down and when I rise up; You understand my thought from afar. You scrutinize my path and my lying down, and are intimately acquainted with all*

my ways. Even before there is a word on my tongue, behold, O LORD, You know it all (Psalm 139:1-4).

5) **Invisible**—to the natural eye and material world
We look not at the things which are seen, but at the things which are not seen; for the things which are seen are temporal, but the things which are not seen are eternal (2 Corinthians 4:18).

He [Jesus] *is the* [visible] *image of the invisible God, the firstborn of all creation: For by Him all things were created, both in the heavens and on earth, visible and invisible* (Colossians 1:15-16).

God is a supernatural being, nearly unfathomable, which separates Him from all other beings—both human and angelic. When we compare His five divine attributes to our own abilities, we might wonder how it is possible for us as mere humans to relate to Him. However, relating to Him is a major need for our maturing process.

As the Eternal One, He does not come to us or go from us as though regulated by the progression of time or limited to a specific location in space. He simply "is." And yet, Scripture teaches us that God relates to each of us in our own lifetimes and localities. To comprehend this, it's necessary to grasp three distinctive characteristics of God:

- He is eternal, not restricted to a past age or future time.
- He is not regulated by natural laws, places, or methods of operation.
- He does not inhabit a particular ethnic race or specific area of the earth.

Our Ever-Present Father

God is the only unchangeable constant. In comparison to the ever-changing natural realm that comes and goes, which becomes and then is no more, God simply "is." As humanity, we deal with a past that has shaped us into who we are today, and we face an unknown future that will add to our development. God is the only dependable constant we can turn to for lasting stability; everything else is changeable.

God is the only dependable constant we can turn to for lasting stability; everything else is changeable.

Has it ever seemed to you that time passes by more quickly as you age? Here's what Neuroscientist David Eagleman said in *The New Yorker* magazine: "This explains why we think that time speeds up when we grow older," Eagleman said, "why childhood summers seem to go on forever, while old age slips by while we're dozing. The more familiar the world becomes, the less information your brain writes down, and the more quickly time seems to pass. Time is this rubbery thing...it stretches out when you really turn your brain resources on, and when you say, 'Oh, I got this; everything is as expected,' it shrinks up." —newyorker.com

The natural realm is in a constant state of change. Today passes and tomorrow comes. What was new becomes old. What did not exist is invented and what is old often ceases to be of useful value. God is the unchangeable constant that never changes, for He "is."

Relational Nature

God is not just a distant super Being who spins galaxies from His fingertips. He has a Father's heart and loves His human offspring more than we can even comprehend.

Consider the power of a father's love for his family. In the following stirring example, Argelia is a 39-year-old mother of two. As a young girl she was ashamed of her dad's job. Like many young people, she didn't realize the many sacrifices he made for her and his family. Now she knows. Her letter to her dad is a beautiful illustration of a father's sacrifice for his family.

> Dear Dad,
>
> Parents often say to their children, "You'll understand when you have kids." I never got that before, but now I feel like that's very true.
>
> Only a parent can understand the sacrifice you made to leave my mom, my sister, and me in Mexico to come work in the United States…Two years later, when we finally moved to the United States to be with you…I didn't understand why you were always working.
>
> But things got real once my classmates started sharing what their parents did for a living. "My dad is a doctor," one said. "My parents own a business," another said. That's when I went home and asked you what you did for a living, and you told me that you were a janitor at a hospital. I was devastated.
>
> At that point, I realized there was absolutely no way I was

going to tell my friends that my dad was a janitor. I avoided the subject for as long as I could before I finally created the lie that you were a scientist.

It wasn't until high school that I started caring less about the opinions of others and more about the great man you were. I learned that many of the same classmates, with dads who were doctors and lawyers, told stories of how these men verbally and physically abused them, abandoned them, ignored them.

For so long, I didn't give you credit for being the man you were and for all of the things you did for us—without fanfare, without complaint, and without rest…Three months before I turned 18 and one year before I became an American citizen, you died after a tragic accident.

Now, I work in the same hospital that you worked in so tirelessly for all those years…. I've never forgotten the lessons you taught me—lessons you probably had no idea you were teaching me. Those lessons changed my life.

—*Argelia*

Can you relate to Argelia's story? It powerfully illustrates a father's love. Her father's devotion to caring and providing for her and her family had gone unnoticed much of the time. If a human father can love this much, how much more does our heavenly Father love us?

The Old Testament gives us a few clues to the relational nature of God as our Father:

> *For You are our Father, though Abraham does not know us and Israel does not recognize us. You, O LORD, are our*

Father, our Redeemer from of old is Your name (Isaiah 63:16).

For a child will be born to us, a son will be given to us; and the government will rest on His shoulders; and His [identifying] *name will be called Wonderful Counselor, Mighty God, Eternal Father, Prince of Peace* (Isaiah 9:6).

Shedding definitive light on the fatherhood of God, when Jesus was born as a son into the natural realm two thousand years ago, he continually called God Father. Jesus always referred to himself not as God but as a son of God. He even instructed us when we pray to address God as, "Our Father who is in heaven."

The multi-faceted nature of God is described in the New Testament as three identifiable personalities: the Father (our relatable source), Jesus (our relatable human example), and the Holy Spirit (our relatable guiding presence).

1. As our Father, God relates to us as our creative source and supplier of all we need.

2. As the son Jesus, God relates to us as the example of His intention for us as children.

3. As the Holy Spirit, God relates to us as our personal guide through life.

It is easier to understand the relational nature of God when we consider the fact that most people, at one time or another, identify and function as a child, a spouse, and a parent. Many times we function in all three roles at the same time.

Take a moment to reflect on your own relationships. They can provide insight into how God relates to us in various roles. God continually functions as a Father, Son, and Holy Spirit, never resting and always available to help us!

Expounding on the character of God, the Bible uses several descriptive titles such as Creator, King, Lord, Judge, Ruler, and Savior. However, the three personalities of Father, Son, and Spirit, are the primary ways we experience a direct relationship with Him.

God is a singular Spirit Being who expresses His love and care for us in multiple ways so we can more fully relate to Him. The Apostle Paul congeals the multiple roles of God in our lives into a simple clarity:

> ...*one God and Father of all, who is over all and through all and in all* (Ephesians 4:5-6).

Loving each of us so fully, His expressive voice came into the natural realm as Jesus Christ, to restore us into the fellowship of His presence.

The Eternal "Is"

God chose Moses to be His representative savior who would facilitate Israel's deliverance from Egyptian captivity. At the beginning of this experience, Moses asked God, "Who shall I say sends me, what is your name?" In response God revealed a descriptive name that adds an insightful depth of clarity regarding His nature, saying:

> *"I AM WHO I AM"* [Hebrew YHWH, pronounced Yahweh]; *and He said, "Thus you shall say to the sons of*

Israel, 'I AM has sent me to you...The LORD, the God of your fathers, the God of Abraham, the God of Isaac, and the God of Jacob, has sent me to you.' This is My name forever...to all generations" (Exodus 3:14-15).

The Hebrew YHWH means to exist, and as a name: Existing One, Ever-Living One, and Eternal One. The name Yahweh was translated into English in the King James' Old Testament about 6800 times as LORD (all caps), about 800 times as GOD (all caps), as Jehovah occasionally, and twice as I Am Who I Am.

When the Hebrews spoke or wrote and repeated a phrase, it was to add emphasis. When God repeated I Am, He in essence said, I Am the One who "is" whenever and however I please. Consider the magnitude of God's declaration. Within or without limitations of time's cycles and progressions, or restrictions of natural appearances, God appears in whatever form He deems appropriate. This revealed name, "I AM WHO I AM" reminds us of what God spoke to John in the book of Revelation:

> *"I am the Alpha and the Omega," says the Lord God, "who is and who was and who is to come, the Almighty"* (Revelation 1:8).

So God told us in both Testaments that He, in a real sense, is the present, the past, and the future all rolled into one. God is time in perfection—inhabiting all time as the present. By definition He said: I Am He Who Is (exists), was (past continuance), and is to come (ever-coming). God basically "is" the Ever-Present One.

As the Ever-Present One, God can intervene in any situation

He chooses because He "is" present at all times, explaining why the verse from Revelation begins with the phrase "who is" before identifying "who was and who is to come." This name speaks of the ageless ONE who IS a guiding presence to all generations, in all ages, and in all of our circumstances. This insight helps us comprehend how the Eternal One relates to us. Unlike His human counterparts, our heavenly Father is always here for us.

> *Be strong and courageous, do not be afraid or tremble at them, for the LORD your God is the one who goes with you. He will not fail you or forsake you* (Deuteronomy 31:6).

Our Free Will

Although the natural realm functions within the limitations of time and space, God does not. He is in all of our beginnings as well as future times. From His vantage point, He can see it all simultaneously. Doesn't this fact amaze you? This is why He knows how our actions affect us and others.

This fact, however, does not mean we are controlled by God or that we are predestined to be or to do anything in particular. While God's sovereign will can override the bad effects of our errors and bring something good out of them, this does not mean that He controls all actions or that everything happens according to His will.

Yes, as Daniel declared, God rules in the affairs of nations, setting up rulers and removing them from power (Daniel 2:20-21). In our individual lives, however, His sovereign will allows us to exercise our God-given free will. Within His sovereignty we are free to do or not, to be godly or not, to bless or cause harm. He allows us to choose and experience the consequences of our choices. Thus we often appear to be cursed or blessed, largely because of our choice.

We often appear to be cursed or blessed, largely because of our choice.

So choose [God's way of] *life in order that you may live, you and your descendants, by loving the LORD your God, by obeying His voice, and by holding fast to Him; for this is your life and the length of your days* (Deuteronomy 30:19-20).

The Eternal I Am who fathers us into existence can appear to be beyond our human ability to relate. Yet He has deposited in each person an eternal part of His Spirit that enables us to sense His presence, hear Him speak, and partake of His eternal way of life:

This is eternal life, that they may know You, the only true God, and Jesus Christ whom You have sent (John 17:3).

His Spoken Word

God is a person and His spoken expression goes forth from His personage. While the person of God and the expressions that proceed from Him are somewhat different, relationally, they are essentially the same. Virtually all of God's expressions, regarding humankind, come through speaking a word. Here are a few examples:

HE CREATES:

Then God said, "Let there be light"; and there was light (Genesis 1:3).

HE RELATES:

The LORD appeared to him from afar, saying, "I have loved you with an everlasting love; therefore I have drawn you with lovingkindness" (Jeremiah 31:3).

HE TRANSFORMS:

A new heart also will I give you, and a new spirit will I put within you: and I will take away the stony heart out of your flesh, and I will give you a heart of flesh (Ezekiel 36:26).

HE INSTRUCTS:

Listen, O my people, to my instruction; incline your ears to the words of my mouth (Psalm 78:1).

HE GUIDES:

Your ears will hear a word behind you, "This is the way, walk in it," whenever you turn to the right or to the left (Isaiah 30:21).

HE INSPIRES:

"Do not worry beforehand about what you are to say, but say whatever is given you in that hour; for it is not [just] *you who speak"* (Mark 13:11).

HE DOES MIRACLES:

He sent His word and healed them, and delivered them from their destructions (Psalm 107:20).

Always existing, God spoke and His expression created the natural universe and mankind. God's spoken expression still goes forth from His essence to create more offspring, and to reform and mature each of "the willing" into His reflective resemblance (image and likeness).

The God who "is" can use a variety of messengers to deliver His thoughts. Occasionally, angelic messengers spoke as though they were God himself. Even more than a messenger, Jesus Christ is the voice (spoken expression) of our Father that uniquely became a visible flesh and blood human, to deliver the illustrated message of God's heart. Jesus' life and his spoken words convey God's mind, will, and desire for our lives.

Ever-Present as the Eternal I AM, God deeply desires to interact and share insights with each of us. As part of our growth and maturing process, He has given us a written word we call Scripture. God's Spirit, as our relatable guiding presence, brings the written word to life and uses it to speak to our hearts today.

Every living person can communicate with the Eternal I AM who, through His interactive presence, is constantly available to all who ask, seek, and knock. Beyond occasional communication with God, our heavenly Father beckons each of us—beckons you—to experience the interactive fellowship with His presence on a daily basis. You can experience intimate encounters with Him as often as you take the time to do so!

Memorize: *"...one God and Father of all, who is over all and through all and in all"* (Ephesians 4:5-6).

Questions for reflection

1. Just how big and majestic is your God?

2. Have you ever felt you were visited by one of God's messengers?

3. Who is the only stable and unchanging constant in life?

Chapter 2

Our Growing Insights

My parents were so in love with God and Scripture that I began to read the Bible as a child. My personal love for Scripture and times with God developed very early. Consequently, during my teenage years, I became very familiar with much of the Bible's content.

During my late teens, we visited a particular church to hear a guest speaker. As the minister touched on different areas of Scripture, I was impressed and followed his thoughts. About 15 minutes into his message, the speaker must have perceived some in the audience looked a bit confused, so he said, "You don't have to understand, just believe it."

The statement caused me to wonder. I began to ponder why God would give us a mind that can reason and understand if He intended us to "just believe." When the phrase was repeated a third time, I concluded that I would not be satisfied with this approach toward God's word. I made a commitment to seek and understand all that God desires to reveal.

I then began the practice of praying as I read Scripture, "Lord, show me what I have not yet seen." My time in Scripture became an insightful road of discovery. Even today, I'll read a passage and sometimes just a verse when an interesting thought will occur, even though I've read the passage countless times before. In many of these moments, I sense God is speaking and sharing new insights. Fresh revelation is a wonderful thing!

When I entertain a fresh thought, many times a confirming passage or event will come to mind. Sometimes a concordance helps me see how a word or phrase is used in other passages. This approach can help bring a clearer understanding of God's intention in the specific verse I'm reading.

Way too often we read into Scripture the perceptions we already have, rather than approach them with a fresh eye and a desire to see and understand what we may not have seen before. The teachings and insights we've already accepted as truth can hinder our ability to perceive or consider fresh perspectives.

So, what thoughts and preconceived ideas do we have about people, groups, the Bible, or even God? Are the opinions you hold formed by truth or by something you may have simply heard over and over again?

Offspring of God

Scripture says we originate in the mind of God and are birthed into the natural realm as offspring of the Spirit of God. When God created the first Adam, He formed a body from earth's dust and infused it with a portion of His Spirit.

All descendants of the first man are endowed with the same spirit of life.

In this world, each of us has a natural body that will eventually return to the dust of the earth and a spirit that returns to God (Ecclesiastes 12:7). No living person is void of God's life-giving Spirit.

We are all birthed as offspring of God who are intended to grow and develop under His guidance into mature children of God. The spirit in each of us equips us with spiritual senses that enable us to hear and receive guidance from our heavenly Father.

The following passage in Acts is quite insightful. (We punctuate the Bible's run-on sentence here for easy reading.)

> *The eternal One made the world and all things in it. Since He is Lord of heaven and earth, God does not dwell in temples made with hands; nor is He served by human hands, as though He needed anything. He Himself gives to all people life and breath and all things. He made from one man every nation of mankind to live on all the face of the earth and determined their appointed times and the boundaries of their habitation. All of this so they would seek Him...though He is not far from each one of us; for in Him we live and move and exist. Even some of your own poets have said, "For we also are His children"* (Acts 17:24-28).

The first parents chose to live another way, and it became an inherited complication to each of their offspring.

God created humanity with the intention of developing us into His image and likeness. Individually, our reflective resemblance (image and likeness) of God is an invitational potential and not necessarily a guarantee. God gives us the freedom to choose when and to what degree we respond to His guidance. When we seek His counsel and respond to His instruction, our potential becomes our developing reality.

> *There was the true Light which, coming into the world, enlightens every man…As many as received Him* [light of Christ], *to them He gave the right to become* [disciplined] *children of God* (John 1:9, 12).

God seeks to enlighten every man and woman. The question is: how receptive are we to His insightful guidance? When we see and hear what our Father is saying and doing and then receive and respond to His counsel, we become better expressions of His heart.

Straying Children

The parable Jesus shared about the Prodigal Son gives us a picture of a son who left his father's care and subsequently returned (Luke 15:11-32). The Prodigal Son chose to enjoy the father's life provision without his father's insightful guidance. Although the son remained an offspring of his father, he ceased to be a child who willingly responded and learned from his father's fairly mature character, attitude, and personality (CAP).

In an uncanny way, the Prodigal Son's story parallels the experience of humanity, as well as our personal separation from God's fellowship. The story illustrates the downward cycle we can experience when we ignore our heavenly Father's insight.

Just like the variables in the Prodigal Son story, some of us are currently walking away from God to spend our inheritance "my way." Some are enjoying a life of riotous living, wasting our gifts and talents on things that don't matter and will eventually pass away. Some are beginning to "lose it" as life starts to fall apart. Some are living in pigpen-like situations, just trying to stay alive.

On the other hand, some are waking up to the realization that we have a heavenly Father and need to repent of our waywardness. Some are amazed at Father's open arms and are experiencing an assurance of His forgiveness. And there are some, like the Prodigal's brother, who stayed home and are still in need of fresh insight into our Father's heart.

The positive and negative movements the Prodigal took can be visualized as a "continuum" in the following chart (to be read in order: -1, -2, etc. and then +1, +2, etc.).

+5 *Continually growing into the fellowship of His presence*
+4 *Receiving and experiencing our Father's love*
+3 *Being amazed at our Father's open arms*
+2 *Repenting of our wayward actions*
+1 *Waking up to the reality of our Father's existence*

-1 *Walking away from God*
-2 *Enjoying a life of riotous living*
-3 *Realizing things are falling apart*
-4 *Trying to survive the pigpen side of life*
-5 *Continuing in a downward spiral away from God's presence*

Our Growing Insights

This chart depicts five progressions away from God and five progressions toward Him. The negative numbers take you further away from God's insightful presence. The positive numbers bring you closer into the experience of His presence. The chart can be adapted to illustrate many situations that take us further from or closer to our Father's fellowship.

As with the Prodigal Son, when we negate the value of spiritual life and our Father's input, we tend to squander the gifting and abilities we are given. Life without the insightful influence of the Father of all spirits tends to be short-changed. On the other hand, those who partake of the fellowship of our Father's presence are blessed with a more abundant life experience.

Can I interrupt for a moment and ask you where you are in this continuum? Are you on the positive side or negative side of this chart? The good news is that wherever you find yourself on this continuum, you can move toward +5, continually growing into our heavenly Father's intention for your life.

Open Minds

God may be displeased with us at times, but He always loves us. His real concern is with our refusal or hesitancy to be influenced by His guidance. The story of the Prodigal Son poignantly illustrates the attitude of God's heart toward repentant offspring and developing children. He is full of grace and mercy, always ready to receive us into His loving arms and share with us the insight we really need.

Don't ever entertain, accept, or believe any thought that says you are worthless or have nothing to contribute. Such thoughts are insults against the Giver of your life. Nothing God makes is worthless, and this applies to every one—including you! There is no sin, no betrayal, and no lapse in devotion that He will not forgive. When we are at our worst, He is at His most loving best. (See my book, *The Christ Culture*, chapter 3.)

> *Or do you think lightly of the riches of His kindness and tolerance and patience, not knowing that the kindness of God leads you to repentance?* (Romans 2:4)

Our personal status as offspring of God is greatly enhanced when we respond as a responsive child to our Father, like Jesus did. When we respond to our Father's guidance, we learn from Him and become better expressions that are more like His own heart.

> *Take My yoke upon you and learn from Me, for I am gentle and humble in heart, and you will find rest for your souls. For My yoke is easy and My burden is light* (Matthew 11:29-30).

God alone is perfect. As offspring and children of God, we are all limited to a developing and maturing process, yet He speaks to us in the midst of our shortcomings and imperfections. The truths God shares with us are much more than a static set of rules or commandments—they are insights that clarify His character, attitude, and personality (CAP). Scripture says the Law was given as a guide that leads us to God's anointing presence.

> *Therefore the Law has become our tutor to lead us to Christ, so that we may be justified by faith. But now that*

Our Growing Insights

faith has come, we are no longer under a tutor. For you are all sons of God through faith in Christ Jesus (Galatians 3:24-26).

Responsive, maturing children under the Father's guidance have no need to function under a strict tutor.

As maturing sons and daughters of our Father, we are much more than subjects of a teacher or distant ruler. We become as children in a close, loving, and intimate fellowship with His presence, where He shares with us temporal and eternal values!

As we follow the guidance God's presence provides, we grow in our perception of Him. The more we understand and learn the ways of Father, the easier it is to move out of our childlike responses in the situations we encounter.

When I was a child, I talked like a child, I thought like a child, I reasoned like a child. When I became a man, I put the ways of childhood behind me (1 Corinthians 13:11).

Maturing children do not think or reason as infants and adolescent children. We learn to view life with a broader perspective and greater understanding. In order to accept the maturing insights God gives and grow in our perceptions and understanding, many times we have to let go of some of our previous ideas and beliefs. We stop thinking as a child.

The disciples provide an example of how previous teachings and experiences can maintain a grip on us. After walking with Jesus for three years and receiving baptizing immersions in His presence, some disciples insisted that followers of Christ accept physical circumcision and observe Jewish food restrictions. The Jewish customs they were taught, before their time with Christ, short-circuited their ability to comprehend the depth of what Jesus clearly taught and demonstrated. (The Jews of that day were even forbidden to have close interaction with non-Jews.)

> *But when Cephas [Peter] came to Antioch, I [Paul] opposed him to his face…For prior to the coming of certain men from James, he used to eat with the Gentiles; but when they came, he began to withdraw and hold himself aloof, fearing the party of the circumcision* (Galatians 2:11-12).

Jesus said the Holy Spirit (God's enabling and anointing presence) would come and guide them into all truth (John 16:13). As insightful as the disciples' walk with Jesus was, they were not able to clearly hear or understand all that God desired to reveal. Jesus said:

> *"I have many more things to say to you, but you cannot bear them now"* (John 16:12).

What we already know and believe can hinder our ability to receive greater depth and clarity.

Their ongoing ability to see, hear, and believe was dependent on their willingness to be open, observe, listen, and allow their beliefs to change and improve. Today, even the most mature among us still see and perceive in part. We want to remember this: what we already know and believe can hinder our ability to receive greater depth and clarity.

Our Growing Insights

There is yet another example in the life of Paul. He was schooled in the Jewish faith by the best religious scholars of his day. Scripture tells us that before his encounter with Christ, Paul was so committed to what he understood to be the will and ways of God that he excelled above his peers.

In the following passage, Paul recounts his first life-changing encounter with Jesus:

> And I said, "Who are You, Lord?" And the Lord said, "I am Jesus whom you are persecuting. But get up and stand on your feet; for this purpose I have appeared to you, to appoint you a minister and a witness not only to the things which you have seen, but also to the things in which I will appear to you" (Acts 26:15-16).

Paul responded to this visitation of Christ and spent the next three years in the desert. (I've noticed that God sometimes leads His children into the wilderness when He wants to re-orient our thought process. Perhaps you find yourself in such a place.) He was already a solid and educated believer in God but was also teachable. As promised, God-in-Christ further appeared to Paul and taught him to think and believe differently.

> But when God...called me through His grace...I did not immediately consult with flesh and blood, nor did I go up to Jerusalem to those who were apostles before me; but I went away to Arabia, and returned once more to Damascus. Then three years later I went up to Jerusalem to become acquainted with Cephas, and stayed with him fifteen days (Galatians 1:15-18).

Years later, Cephas (Peter) said Paul's understanding of the Gospel was beyond his own.

> *Our beloved brother Paul, according to the wisdom given him, wrote to you, as also in all his letters…in which are some things hard to understand* (2 Peter 3:15-16).

Why? Paul received a clearer perception and understanding of God's intent than Peter was able to comprehend. Peter was still struggling with his past teachings and perceptions, so the fresher and clearer insights Paul received from the Spirit of Truth were problematic to him.

Our particular view of God, Scripture, and life in general affects the attitudes we project and the way we react to situations. If we have declared our views a few times, our commitment to them can be nearly unbreakable. We can be so committed to what we've proclaimed that a different view can even cause us to feel threatened as though our integrity is being called into question. Too often our ability to perceive the fresh insights God shares are hindered by what we already believe.

New Possibilities

Consider what makes inventors successful. How do they come up with what was not previously seen or known? Inventors first tend to consider new thoughts and insights as possibilities and then proceed to work through the details of creating what has not already existed. Their current understanding of the way things work does not prevent them from exploring new possibilities.

George Washington Carver was one such individual. It is

Our Growing Insights

said he came up with 300 uses for the peanut and more than 120 uses for the sweet potato. At the time, everyone knew about the obvious use of these two crops as food staples. Why look any further? Carver's motivation was to encourage further planting of peanuts and sweet potatoes to promote crop rotation with cotton. By identifying more uses and formulating a larger market demand, farmers would be more likely to plant these two crops. So the known was set aside while the possible was considered.

It is said that Steve Jobs redefined five separate industries, one of which is the cell phone. In 2007, Apple's launch of the iPhone propelled smartphones into the mainstream, thanks to the device's attractive design and intuitive user interface. It was the first commercial smartphone to use finger input as its main means of interaction, instead of a stylus, physical keyboard, or keypad.

While Jobs did not technically invent the smartphone, he envisioned a world where people used a handheld device to communicate and compute. As a result, today we can make phone calls and check our bank balances, listen to our music libraries, even watch live TV on our smartphones—all because someone thought there could be more.

God invites us to look beyond our history, beyond what was or even is, and consider the additional insights He may be revealing today. We should all ask, is our view of truth a bit limiting or no longer appropriate? As our life changes, our reaction to the season we are in may require us to consider new possibilities. Don't let your current perceptions fog your ability to see and hear afresh.

> *For we know in part...but when the perfect* [mature] *comes, the partial will be done away...For now we see in a mirror dimly...now I know in part* (1 Corinthians 13:9-12).

God has even designed our natural life process to draw us into greater levels of maturity and godly behavior. When we marry we begin to learn more intently that life is not all about me but about us. When we become parents, we discover us includes children. More often than not, me becomes very secondary to the needs of our children. When we become grandparents, our circle of concern and devotion again changes.

Has there been a point in your life when your perception of God began to change from that of being a harsh Judge who is ready to condemn, to being a gracious Savior who lovingly forgives. Have you begun to realize God is more than a King who rules the universe, that He is your loving and insightful Father? You may want to ask yourselves what additional insights God desires to reveal to you. Are you growing or are you dying in stagnation?

God wants us to receive His guidance and be willing to follow His lead, day-by-day and season-by-season. This requires that we remain soft, flexible, teachable, and open to receive and embrace His fresh influence in each new situation and circumstance.

When God instructed Abraham to sacrifice his son Isaac, Abraham correctly believed God wanted him to kill Isaac as a worshipful offering:

> *Now it came about...that God tested Abraham, and said to him, "Abraham!" And he said, "Here I am." He said,*

"Take now your son, your only son, whom you love, Isaac, and go to the land of Moriah, and offer him there as a burnt offering" (Genesis 22:1-2).

When Abraham proceeded to do as asked, God countered His previous instruction:

Abraham stretched out his hand and took the knife to slay his son. But the angel of the Lord called to him from heaven and said, "Abraham, Abraham!" And he said, "Here I am." He said, "Do not stretch out your hand against the lad, and do nothing to him; for now I know that you fear [reverence] *God"* (Genesis 22:10-12).

We also want to be attentive and flexible enough to hear God speak.

God's instructive and guiding word to us can change! As with Abraham, God's maturing intent is not always obvious with our first perception or our current understanding. While we want to commit ourselves to following God's instruction, we also want to be attentive and flexible enough to hear God speak afresh, rather than stick to a previous perception that is no longer appropriate.

Since our capacity as offspring and children of God living in the natural realm is somewhat limited, our comprehensions of what God is saying and doing, are at best, limited. We will never be as complete as He is, in essence or in understanding.

Everything we perceive and know is in part. As children, we can only relate to the insights we are able to see, hear, and comprehend.

A Greater Perspective

The world we live in today is filled with prejudice, snap judgements, and reactionary attitudes. Brothers are pitted against brothers, churches compete against churches, and political parties revile each other.

To really understand something, it is often helpful to examine its parts. Dissecting and dividing the elements of a unit into its separate components can allow a better understanding to emerge of the whole unit. To really understand the unit, however, we must put all the elements back together and look at them as a complete whole. As a unit, the functional purpose of parts becomes more obvious.

You may remember the story of the six blind men feeling different parts of an elephant and drawing conclusions about an elephant from each of their separate viewpoints? The person feeling a leg, for example, thought the elephant as a whole was exactly like the single part he was experiencing.

Viewing the individual parts of anything without seeing how they fit and function together, can result in an incomplete understanding. This may be so whether we are viewing an object, a person, God, or the purposes and ways of our heavenly Father. Our function as parts of one another helps bring clarity to our individual purpose.

Social perception is the result of our forming opinions of

others. These opinions can be based on physical appearance, apparent personality, observed behavior, and other factors. There is a TV commercial that shows a biker-type who angrily states, "I want them dead!" This is disturbing until you see the biker holding a small dog and speaking to a veterinarian. The commercial is for a product to kill fleas and ticks!

How quick we are to judge people by momentary impressions, outward appearances, and simple characteristics! Doing so can hinder our ability to see beyond the obvious in order to appreciate their inner qualities. Long held beliefs, perceptions, and prejudices can hinder our ability to properly relate to each other and to scriptural truth. When we focus on differences as contrasting characteristics instead of complementary values, confusion and destructive reactions can result.

To understand the truth of Scripture, we want to examine the individual books and verses. But then we need to consider how the separate insights and perspectives blend and merge into a relational wholeness.

Around 500 years ago, Martin Luther decided to become a priest. Because of his training in the Law, he was trained to be a Church scholar and theologian. When he began to declare what he found in Scripture, contrary to official doctrine, he was put on trial for treason against the Church. In response he proclaimed: "Unless I am convinced by proofs from Scriptures or by plain and clear reasons and arguments, I can and will not retract." While reading Scripture, Luther discovered many official doctrines did not make good scriptural sense. Reason has a part to play in our faith in God.

In order to understand the character, mannerisms, and ways

of God, we must remember to put all the pieces together and view God as a complete Being.

An example can be observed in discussions about God being one, two, or three Persons. Whichever viewpoint you happen to embrace, we can all agree that God reveals Himself to us as our Father, as His spoken expression that was incarnated to live for a time as a human, and as an anointing presence of Spirit. Each is an expression of God that comes from His being.

Ineffectiveness also happens when we approach truth and divide it into a spiritual or physical application. In this life, reality involves both the spiritual and physical elements of our being operating in tandem. We do nothing that is exclusively spiritual or natural because we are spirit and flesh. (See chapter 2 in *Created to Relate.*)

We do nothing that is exclusively spiritual or natural because we are spirit and flesh.

Another example can be noted. When we view the justice of God, we must remember that His primary characteristic is love. His justice is administered as the disciplinary actions of a loving Father. God does not react out of anger, nor does He seek revenge or punish us just because we deserve it. The judgments of God are actually corrective expressions of the grace and mercy of God upon those who do not willingly accept His instructive guidance.

Our Growing Insights

> *"My son, do not regard lightly the discipline* [training instruction] *of the Lord, nor faint when you are reproved by Him; for those whom the Lord loves He disciplines"...It is for discipline that you endure; God deals with you as with sons; for what son is there whom his father does not discipline?* (Hebrews 12:5-7)

Rightly Discern

Dividing Scripture into Old and New Testament perspectives can negate the rich validity the Old provides for our New Testament world. Scripture rightly states that we are, in many ways, what we think (Proverbs 23:7). We do not want to remain the same and become stagnant. Stagnation is a stale condition that breeds infection and produces destructive effects.

It is important that we remain pliable enough to at least consider new insight as fresh water being poured into our pond, lest we quit learning, growing, developing, and maturing. Our quest should always be to at least consider more than what we currently understand as we seek to clearly see where God is leading us.

> *But the path of the righteous is like the light of dawn, that shines brighter and brighter until the full day* (Proverbs 4:18).

Solomon, said to be the wisest of all men, declared there is wisdom in a multitude of counselors. This is why it is good to discuss and share with each other what we are sensing and hearing. Let us consider one another's insights and perceptions as possible complements to our own spiritual growth.

If you are not accustomed to deep discussions with others about the issues of life, try this experiment: Get together with at least one other person, preferably two, and talk about the subject of this chapter—the value of embracing new ideas vs. holding on to current understandings. You just might be surprised by the outcome!

Memorize: *But the path of the righteous is like the light of dawn that shines brighter and brighter until the full day* (Proverbs 4:18).

Questions for reflection:

1. Inventors envision new ideas and concepts. Have you ever had a fresh or new idea?

2. Should we only think and believe what we have been taught? Why or why not?

3. Why does the word spoken to us by the Eternal I Am occasionally change?

Chapter 3

True Light of Our Life

As a young man I found life to be full of interesting variables. My curiosity about life sharpened as I became aware of others and something of a student of people. I listened to what people said and watched what they did. I learned to carefully listen and observe, and tried to put two and two together in an effort to make sense of it all.

My parents encouraged me to have a personal relationship with God from early childhood. As a result, I grew up reading Scripture, learning about God and responding to His influencing presence. It had a significant effect on my developing understanding of life, and it greatly influenced how I acted.

As a pre-teen, I repeatedly committed myself to God and His way of life. My desire to know God and learn from Him kept me listening and observing to see and hear what God was saying and doing. I was truly blessed to have such a focus early in life.

One evening during my early teens, while walking to my job at a local restaurant, I recalled some of the dramatic conversion stories I had recently heard. Many testimonies recounted the graphic experiences people had when they first turned to God or when they returned to Him. During my walk I began to wonder if I was missing out by not having a dramatic conversion.

I asked God, "Should I walk away from Your fellowship, so I can experience such a wonderful conversion?" Almost immediately I sensed God say to me, "You have chosen the better way." There's no telling how much pain and suffering I avoided because I chose to continue to seek the fellowship of His presence.

Two Sources of Wisdom

In the Garden of Eden, God provided an environment that made available everything His newly created children needed to grow and develop, both physically and spiritually. Their days in this natural realm included a vast array of options—they could choose a variety of foods to eat, things to do, and places to roam.

The spirit that God infused into Adam, giving life to the formed body, equipped him with five senses so he could see, hear, perceive, and partake of both the natural and spiritual realities. What God used to form Eve was taken from Adam so she had all these aptitudes and all their children inherited them as well. We are as they were, designed to grow and mature by simultaneously partaking of both the natural and spiritual realities.

> *Out of the ground the LORD God caused to grow every tree that is pleasing to the sight and good for food; the tree of life also in the midst of the garden, and the tree of the knowledge of good and evil…but from the tree of the knowledge of good and evil you shall not eat, for in the day that you eat from it you will surely die* (Genesis 2:9, 17).

Out of all the things to eat and do, God restricted only one, saying it would bring deathly side effects. When they chose to partake of what was both forbidden and ill advised, they chose to set aside God's guidance and seek wisdom by this other source.

> *When the woman saw that the tree was good for food, and that it was a delight to the eyes, and that the tree was desirable to make one wise, she took from its fruit and ate; and she gave also to her husband with her, and he ate* (Genesis 3:6).

We ask, what was this restricted source of insight and wisdom they chose to experience? Scripture describes their wrongful choice as "a tree of knowledge" that was encouraged by a tempting serpent with a deceitful thought. Their life changed as their eyes were opened to see differently. Negating God's guidance, they began to learn and become wise another way.

Was the death God spoke of, a result of "disobeying" His instruction? Or was it a result of what they chose to "partake of" that became a part of their maturing growth? The answer is not one or the other but both. We generally focus on disobedience and overlook the later part of the equation. What did they choose to "look to" for wisdom?

The Overlooked

Both of these special trees were God-given resources that were identified as good and pleasing. They were specifically placed in the midst of the garden as core or central provisions. The restricted one, in and of itself, was not fully a bad thing; remember, God placed it in their midst. When we look further into Scripture, we find each of these trees were sources of insight and wisdom that would support and nourish their development. Let's examine each, starting with the Tree of Life.

> *In the beginning was the Word, and the Word...was in the beginning with God...In Him was life, and the life was the light of men* (John 1:1, 4).
>
> *Concerning the Word of Life—and the life was manifested* [made visible], *and we have seen and testify and proclaim to you the eternal life, which was with the Father and was manifested to us* (1 John 1:1-2).
>
> *...A river of the water of life, clear as crystal, coming from the throne of God...On either side of the river was the tree of life...Blessed are those who wash their robes* [in repentance], *so that they may have the right to the tree of life* (Revelations 22:2, 14).

The tree of life in the Garden clearly represents a readily available deposit of the word of God. This tree was a visual of God's expressive voice and written Scripture; both support spiritual life. Today, His nourishing words of life are readily available to each of us in the form of His still small voice. Every expression that comes from God provides nourishing life and light to our lives. All who partake of this source are truly blessed.

Realizing the Tree of Life is much more than a natural tree, we turn our attention toward the other source of wisdom placed in the midst, which was also more than a natural tree. We begin by asking; what does Scripture mean when it uses the word "good"?

> *Every good thing given and every perfect gift is from above, coming down from the Father of lights* (James 1:17).

> *Therefore do not let what is for you a good thing be spoken of as evil; for the kingdom of God is…righteousness and peace and joy in the Holy Spirit* (Romans 14:16-17).

These passages and many others point out two important insights: 1) All good comes from God; and 2) He allows us to make a choice within the good.

As part of our maturing growth, God expects us to exercise the free will He has given us. This is important. When we hear His advice, we are free to receive and adapt the good of His wisdom to our slightly different situations and circumstances, to find our personal level of right and peace within the good He provides. God's good is not rigid, hard, destructive, or unadaptable. God allows us, as His children, to grow and mature at our own pace. He is such an understanding Father!

Now let's consider the scriptural use of the word "evil." The Hebrew word is *ra,'* which is an adjective that means: an inferior quality; as mischievous, injurious, severely harmful.

Simply put, ra' speaks of severe, injurious activity and destructive behavior. This defines what Scripture calls evil.

At first glance, this tree of the knowledge of good and evil appears to present contrasting values. But Scripture does not say, good "or" evil; it says good "and" evil. The values are not contrasted with "or"; they are allied with "and." This tree is a complex composite.

So we ask, how can God's good be associated with and in collusion with a destructive element? Simply, when the good is taken to extremes, the extreme application becomes harmful, destructive, deadly, and evil. Examples of these extremes are socialism and Communism, which take the biblical perspectives of sharing and commonality to extremes by forcing compliance. Other extremes may be the staunch liberal and conservative ideologies that take a view of an issue too far in one direction.

Seek after that which is good for one another and for all people (1 Thessalonians 5:15).

In our efforts to protect or amplify a good, we tend to take a good and create laws and binding restrictions that require compliance. In turn, this becomes destructive to the exercise of our God-given free will. The good God provides is not intended to be laws that require obedience. Laws can be as overlords that hold us captive and negate the maturing value that develops when we freely choose. Consequently, requiring "too much of a good thing" speaks of excess!

The natural laws of nature are quite absolute: for example, every action causes a reaction, thus gravity draws and fire burns. However, spiritual instructions are not like natural laws. The spiritual is not limited or restricted to the absolutes found in the laws of nature. Spiritual truth involves everything in relationship, it is not "this or that" but each working together.

The spiritual is not limited or restricted to the absolutes found in the laws of nature.

Rigid laws tend to demand compliance rather than encouraging a willing response. Our efforts to force others into the good rather than offering it in appealing ways can cause the good to appear as destructive restrictions. Does this approach toward God and His ways have any bearing on why many unbelievers are repelled rather than drawn to the Christian faith? The excessive extremes of this source of wisdom produce quite a contrast with the balance provided in the Tree of Life.

Have you ever noticed that people tend to react negatively when you've confronted them with a word of correction? Have you ever reacted defensively when the rebuke is directed toward you? But what happens when the correction is offered as an appealing suggestion or as a better idea? More often than not, people respond more positively when new ideas or corrections are presented gently rather than aggressively and then given time to sink in. Might be something you want to consider.

Another example is found in "ego." During our human beginnings, a deception twisted God's stated purpose for us to insinuate we are supposed to be "as God," something more than offspring of God (Genesis 3:4-5; 2 Corinthians 11:3). Adam and Eve's acceptance of the scam planted in them an overly strong inclination toward self-centeredness, my importance as an inflated view of "me, myself and I." An example of extremes is found in the phrase, "my way or the highway."

As a result, we all inherit an overly strong focus on our own importance. While everyone has contributing value and our self-awareness as a person is important, an inflated ego is an extreme and can be quite destructive. Before the inflated self-centered ego brought separation and became Adam and Eve's norm, they are described as being without shame, excuse, blame, or cover-up (Genesis 2:25). They only knew of God's peaceful and balancing relational concept.

As they chose to ignore and thus negate the value of God's spoken word, Adam and Eve embarked on a path of learning from extremes, mostly through the ill side effects of trial and error, rather than by the peaceful results that can come from instruction.

A Deadly Decision

Keep in mind, God planted this tree as a source of nutrition and said it was good. The restriction He gave was to help solidify their resolve to learn and gain wisdom through His guidance. God instructed Adam and Eve to abstain from learning from the extremes experienced in trial and error, warning that partaking of it results in deathly side effects.

> *From any tree of the garden you may eat freely; but from the tree of the knowledge of good and evil you shall not eat, for in the day that you eat from it you will surely die* (Genesis 2:16-17).

An interesting insight is found in the wording of this passage. The Hebrew translated "die" in this text is the indefinite tense, which linguistically indicates "ing" should be added to the English equivalent. This is important because this cautionary instruction speaks of an ongoing process. This passage actually says, for during the time you partake, you will be dying.

The above verse does not address the eventual death of the body. The physical death was always part of God's plan, as a means of advancing us into the next life, into the eternal realm. This caution was to keep them from ongoing death experiences, in various degrees and levels of lifelessness, which are a result of trial and error.

For example, in the early nineteenth century, arsenic was often used to commit murder. It was readily available as rat poison and symptoms of arsenic poisoning were similar to those of common maladies so it was easy to misdiagnose. Although recipients knew they were sick, victims were not aware they were slowly being poisoned. When small amounts of the arsenic were poured into their system over time, they began a slow ongoing death.

Adam and Eve's feeding at the "tree of extremes" created in them and in all humanity, an inclination toward learning and attaining wisdom through trial and error, rather than through the fellowship of God's spoken expressions; via the Tree of Life.

There are also positive examples of the value of trial and error as provided in the following story. However, in most life situations God's best involves hearing His voice rather than suffering the ill (deathly) side effects that can accompany learning by experience.

"I have not failed. I've just found 10,000 ways that won't work." —*Thomas A. Edison*

What Edison also said, according to an 1890 interview in *Harper's Monthly Magazine* was, "I speak without exaggeration when I say that I have constructed three thousand different theories in connection with the electric light, each one of them reasonable and apparently true. Yet only in two cases did my experiments prove the truth of my theory."

This means Edison tried roughly 3000 experiments that failed to produce his desired result: a practical, commercially viable electric bulb. (It should be noted that Edison did not invent the first light bulb, but the forerunners to his invention only burned for a few hours at best.) Edison's bulb, for which he was awarded a US Patent in 1880, lasted 50 to 60 days. This difference made his light bulb a commercially viable alternative to gas lamps, kerosene lamps, and wax candles.

Edison's experimental method is referred to as trial and error. Back in the day, he was often criticized for his methods. In defense of his approach to inventing, Edison stated that the underlying science on which he might have based his experiments did not yet exist. Therefore he was forced to hunt for possible filament materials for his light bulb and keep trying until one of those worked. There was no one to instruct him since no such invention had ever existed before this time.

This quote, attributed to Thomas Edison, illustrates the point of this chapter. Contrasted with Edison's circumstances, many of us only learn by trial and error because we undervalue instruction. In either case we will learn something. However, learning by instruction will usually get us to the desired end result much quicker and with less pain and suffering. Unlike Edison, who was forced to use trial and error to invent a better light bulb, we have the shared experience of parents, teachers, written Scripture, and God's still small voice to illuminate our path.

In life, there are many examples of perfecting a skill by trial and error: refining a recipe, creating a design, writing a book, or learning how to play golf. We could say these are appropriate pursuits of learning. Conversely, there are other skills that do not lend themselves to the trial and error method: for example, learning to drive a car, and learning to fly a helicopter. These skills require the help of an instructor. They are just too dangerous to learn on our own.

Dying But Not Alone

The decision our first parents made in the Garden was not the better way to pursue learning. Choosing against God's best dulled their spiritual senses, thereby hindering their ability to clearly hear God speak and to sense eternal spiritual truth. The impaired ability to see and hear God speak was evidenced by their actions.

> *They heard the sound of the LORD God walking in the garden in the cool of the day, and the man and his wife hid themselves* (Genesis 3:8).
>
> *Your iniquities have made a separation between you and your God, and your sins have hidden His face from you* (Isaiah 59:2).

It's important to note: they were still able to see God and hear Him speak, even in their sin, for He appeared and conversed with them. However, their ability to clearly see and comprehend Him was compromised. Following Adam and Eve's bad choice, all humanity entered a state of existence that leans toward learning through the not-so-good process of trial and error. This tree was a God provision, but was not the preferred choice.

While God sent them out of the Garden environment to experience what they chose, God did not abandon them to their choice. He came to them after their divisive error. His presence also came to their children, Cain and Abel, and multitudes throughout history. He is still appealing to each of us today to accept the fellowship of His insightful presence.

Although God still speaks and we can hear His guidance, too often we misinterpret what we hear or ignore the instruction. We rely more heavily on what our past experience has taught and suffer the destructive side effects of our choices.

The process of learning through trial and error produces many ups and downs, good times and trying times. Some of our not-so-good experiences involve fights, arguments, and even wars between peoples and nations. The negative results are generally very unpleasant, producing hurts, broken hearts, scars, and discouragement. Yes, while experience can be a good teacher, it is often not the best way.

We all agree experience can be a good teacher. However, God offers another way. When we ignore God's word of instruction and prefer to learn through the experience of trial and error, life includes many ill side effects of error, destructive extremes, and deadly experiences. The result for us today is that we are living below our intended abundance.

A Remedy

Since God, as a loving Father, created this natural realm with all its variables and possibilities for our growing development, He also provides a remedy for the problems we encounter in our trial and error. God can bring a beneficial result out of our negative experiences.

> *And we know that God causes all things to work together for good to those who love God, to those who are called according to His purpose* (Romans 8:28).

If Adam and Eve had repented of their sin (acknowledged their error and chose to ask for forgiveness), God's forgiving nature would have helped them adjust and remain in close fellowship with His presence. God's grace and mercy, nevertheless, reached out to help by removing them from the Garden while they were unrepentant, lest they remain in that condition. Our access to the Tree of Life is only restricted by our lack of repentance.

Our access to the Tree of Life is only restricted by our lack of repentance.

Similarly the parable of the Prodigal Son is a picture of humanity through the ages—choosing to do things one's own way instead of God's way. The Prodigal took his father's provision, left the father's influence, and squandered his inheritance on undisciplined living.

Humanity still leans toward the ill effects of life guided by the good and evil of trial and error. We suffer from the same tendency to ignore God's guiding presence.

> *Who dwell in darkness and in the shadow of death…because they rebelled against the words of God and spurned the council of the Most High* (Psalm 107:10-11).

Too often, the inferior perspective of learning on our own keeps us confused about God's love and care. And when things do not go well, we cry, "Why is this happening?" or "Why does God allow this?" The pains of trial and error are not the best way to learn.

Conversely, God intends that we hear and follow His instruction, and partake of the tree of life (satisfying fulfillment) provided by His life-supporting voice and abiding presence.

> *As many as received Him* [God-in-Christ], *to them He gave the right to become* [disciplined] *children of God* (John 1:12).

We do not have to live our lives devoid of the insight of God's presence. Each of us can see and hear God speak. We can all listen to what God is saying and observe what He is doing. While we are accustomed to using trial and error, it's never too late to choose God's better way. He is not hesitant to welcome us into the fellowship of His presence.

> *Now therefore, O sons, listen to me, for blessed are they who keep my ways. Heed instruction and be wise, and do*

not neglect it. Blessed is the man who listens to me, watching daily at my gates, waiting at my doorposts. For he who finds me finds life and obtains favor from the LORD (Proverbs 8:32-35).

When Adam and Eve separated themselves from their Father's guidance and began to live as the Prodigal Son, they compromised their status as instructed children and became as mere offspring. They even began to think as though they were supposed to learn solely from their mistakes. Such a life, separated from God's guidance, tends to produce the godless actions and deathly lifestyles we still see and experience today.

Spiritual Life

God invites each of us to partake of His interactive fellowship, during this life. We are birthed into this earth, intending that we utilize all our natural and spiritual faculties.

We are designed to grow, develop, and mature into God's reflection and resemblance (image and likeness). Without His input, however, our maturing growth is greatly hampered. While we can develop and obtain levels of wisdom by ignoring God's input, doing so has its drawbacks and deathly side effects. Remember, God restricted access to the tree of the knowledge of good and evil, not because it was a bad thing, but because it was not the better way.

When we become aware that God is our Father and become receptive to His fatherly influence, we learn to live with His perspective. As we hear and respond to the voice of God, we partake of the Tree of Life—the living expression of God that was manifested in Jesus Christ.

But as many as received Him, to them He gave the right to become children (John 1:12).

The life we are designed to live on this earth involves both natural and spiritual realities that function in harmony. While our body comes from the natural earth and enables us to communicate with the natural realm, our spirit comes from the Eternal I Am and enables us to communicate with the spiritual realm and our heavenly Father. God intends that we learn, not so much by trial and error, but by actively partaking of the fellowship of His guiding presence. This is spiritual life!

God has given us eternal life, and this life is in His Son (1 John 5:11).

This is eternal life, that they may know You, the only true God, and Jesus Christ whom You have sent (John 17:3).

As we experience God's presence, we partake of the eternal quality of life that comes from Him. We all need the loving guidance of God's presence, to assist our growth and development beyond our current level of maturity. The choice is ours to make!

I encourage you to cultivate your sensitivity to the spiritual realm and God's presence throughout the day. One way to do this is to pause frequently for reflection, prayer, or simply acknowledging His closeness.

Memorize: *This is eternal life, that they may know You, the only true God, and Jesus Christ whom You have sent* (John 17:3).

Questions for reflection:

What were the two sources of wisdom God provided in the Garden?

What does the Tree of Life represent?

What does the tree of the knowledge of good and evil represent?

Chapter 4

Learn From Ancient Experiences

From my early teens into my mid-twenties, my parents and I, along with one or more of my four brothers, traveled the country, visiting one ministry after another. It seemed like we were on the road constantly. The continual movement was not a normal way to raise a family. Relatives who were watching our movements said they didn't know what to think. Occasionally we'd hear them say, "We never know if you are coming or going."

Schooling for us boys was something of a roller-coaster ride. During my eighth grade I started classes in California. A month later we were in Texas and I breezed through classes because they were a bit behind California's curriculum. Mid-year we were in Indiana and I was barely able to keep up. During the last two months of the school year, we were back in California and I was struggling to catch up. Then, two weeks before graduation, we were on the road again.

Learn From Ancient Experiences

During these years we anticipated the imminent return of Jesus. We, like many others at the time, believed His return would immediately change believers and equip us to rule and reign with Christ. Education was not considered a high priority, perhaps even a waste of time. Nevertheless, I developed a desire to understand.

While growing up this way did not allow me to develop close friendships, it taught me to be pliable and moldable. While I knew what I knew, my experience caused me to keep an open mind and be flexible. I learned to accept the fact that, in this life, things change and pass away while the eternal perspectives we adapt has lasting effects on us.

As a lifestyle, our family read and studied Scriptures daily. We traveled across the country with two driving perspectives. On the one hand, we intensely sought to respond to God's leading and learn of Him. On the other hand, we looked with great anticipation for the imminent return of Christ, which would miraculously change and equip us to rule and reign with Him. There appeared to be no conflict between these two emphases because both concepts were widely taught at the time.

Eventually, I realized that God will not miraculously change and mature anyone in a moment of time. We progressively mature while interacting with His presence. I encourage you to not stop your spiritual growth at reading about others' theories and experiences—including those shared in this book. Put what you learn to work, in your own life and relationships! Your experience will add enriching depth to your life process.

Our Beginnings

While God created the vast natural universe, He parented the first man and woman. Fatherhood originated with God and He obviously knows how to be the ideal Father. As good as any natural father may be, our heavenly Father is many times better. God says He is involved in our individual making, forming, and gifting even in our mother's womb.

Scripture tells us in the book of Genesis that God made the first human with both natural and spiritual components. The first human body was formed from natural realm elements and was infused with life from God's Spirit. Under the creative hand of God, this body and spirit combination produced a conscious soul with the ability to be self-aware and relate to others, in both the natural and spiritual realms.

My book, *Created to Relate*, provides an interesting look into the wonders of our human makeup. In an easy to read manner, it examines the difference in what we are as a being and who we are as a person. It unveils the scriptural perspective of how each of our components functions, interacts, and then clarifies why we exist. Our function as individuals makes each of us different and uniquely special. I recommend you get a copy and add it to your "must read" list.

The first man and woman were equipped with five senses (sight, hearing, touch, taste, and smell). Their senses enabled them to detect what was happening in both the natural and spiritual realms. As offspring of the first parents, we have the same makeup. Each person is equipped with the same ability to see, hear, and sense both natural and spiritual activity. We all experience spiritual realities in various degrees and at different levels of awareness.

Our heavenly Father is involved in each of our beginnings. This is true even if the conditions of our conception are not ideal. No one is brought into this life purely by human action. We all go through the same creative process in our mother's womb, despite the activity of our natural parents. God has a hand in each of our lives, forming and bringing into life His additional offspring with the potential of becoming mature children of God!

Our heavenly Father is involved in each of our beginnings.

Thus says the LORD, your Redeemer, and the one who formed you from the womb, "I, the LORD, am the maker of all things" (Isaiah 44:24).

You formed my inward parts; You wove me in my mother's womb (Psalm 139:13).

Each of us has some qualities of our heavenly Father's nature—but no one has all of them. So it is with human offspring, no child has all their parents' qualities. Parents can pass on a person's hair color, physical build, intelligence, or some special gifting such as musical or artistic ability—or not. The DNA we inherit explains this phenomenon.

Roughly fifty percent of our DNA comes from each of our parents. In turn, each of them received 50% of their DNA from their parents. That means we are birthed with 25% of our DNA from our grandparents—and so on. Even so, we are not exact copies of our ancestors. Some genetic traits are expressed and some are considered recessive, meaning they may not be obvious in us but might be expressed in one or more of our offspring (source: Ancestry.com).

While each of our mothers and fathers are different and play a big role in contributing to our overall make-up, we are more than simply a compilation of our natural parents. Many of the gifts and talents we are born with come from our parents, but it is also obvious that our parents are not the only contributors to our uniqueness.

> *For the gifts and the calling of God are irrevocable* (Romans 11:29).

Our heavenly Father parents each of us as expressions of His heart, designed to live as His children. Adam and Eve's experience in the Garden of Eden demonstrates that God's creative intention was not fully realized during their Garden experience. As with Adam and Eve, His image and likeness (reflection and resemblance) is intended for us but is not yet accomplished. We are all a work in process.

Experience of the Ages

Someone once said, "A man with experience is not at a disadvantage to a man with a theory." Experiences have a way of enriching and adding depth to our understanding. The things we experience of a natural and a spiritual nature add to our

Learn From Ancient Experiences

developing maturity. When we hear what God is saying and go where He is leading, our personal experience becomes part of our maturing journey and helps anchor us in greater understanding of both realities.

Our Bible is a compilation of writings that relate people's interaction with God. It records for us their responses to the insights, provisions, and relationship He offers. Scripture usually mentions the method God used to convey His message. Sometimes people heard an audible voice or received an inspiring thought. Many times they heard God speak through a prophet or an angel. Other times God appeared in a dream or a day vision. Once, it is recorded that God spoke through a donkey. (See Numbers 22:22-34.)

Scriptural accounts of God visiting and speaking are obviously not the only times people experienced the presence of God. The biblical accounts are just a mere sampling of the ways and the areas in life where God shares insightful guidance and blessing.

Let's look at thirteen of the many examples where God's presence came to speak and provide direction to people regarding numerous situations they experienced. This is not an exhaustive list; it just shares some of the more notable accounts. We have labeled them to amplify some of the different areas He offers insightful help to our lives.

As you read this list, I encourage you to open your mind and heart to an expanded view of God's presence and interaction in your life. If you haven't already, I urge you to go beyond simply knowing His saving presence, as in number 4 below, to experience the many other possibilities of God's deep connection to your life.

1. **A Conversing Presence:** Adam and Eve are identified as our first human parents. In the New Testament, Paul said we all came from this one parentage (Acts 17:26). God's presence came to fellowship with them both before and after they disobeyed.

> *Then the LORD God formed man of dust from the ground, and breathed into his nostrils the breath of life; and man became a living being* (Genesis 2:7).
>
> *Then the LORD God said, "It is not good for the man to be alone; I will make him a helper* [a complement] *suitable for him"* (Genesis 2:18).
>
> *They heard the sound of the LORD God walking in the garden…and the man and his wife hid themselves from the presence of the LORD God* (Genesis 3:8).

2. **An Instructive Presence:** Cain was Adam and Eve's firstborn son. God's presence came to offer him insight about the source of his anger toward Abel. When Cain refused God's word of caution, he remained angry, became spiteful, and turned away from Him.

> *The LORD said to Cain, "Why are you angry…If you do well, will not your countenance be lifted up? And if you do not do well, sin is crouching at the door; and its desire is for you, but you must master it"…Cain rose up against Abel his brother and killed him…Then Cain went out from the presence of the LORD* (Genesis 4:6-8, 16).

3. **A Transforming Presence:** Enoch was the 7th generation from Adam. When Enoch was 65, he responded to God's presence and walked with Him for the rest of his life. Their

fellowship was so intense that Enoch was translated into the eternal realm, bypassing death.

> *Then Enoch walked with God...after he became the father of Methuselah...So all the days of Enoch were three hundred and sixty-five years. Enoch walked with God; and he was not, for God took him* (Genesis 5:22-23).

4. A Saving Presence: Noah appears in the 3rd generation from Enoch. God spoke and instructed him to build an Ark to save Noah and his family from the destructive flood that was coming upon the earth. Take notice that his righteousness was the exercise of faith.

> *By faith Noah, being warned by God about things not yet seen, in reverence prepared an ark for the salvation of his household...and became an heir of the righteousness which is according to faith* (Hebrews 11:7).

5. A Revealing Presence: Abraham appears in the 7th generation after Enoch. He heard God speak to him when he was 75 years old. Scripture records him interacting with the presence of God at least nine times (Genesis chapters 12–22). Abraham's faithful response resulted in him being called the father of all the faithful.

> *No longer shall your name be called Abram, but your name shall be Abraham; for I have made you the father of a multitude of nations* (Genesis 17:5).

> *For this reason it is by faith...in order that the promise will be guaranteed to all...those who are of the faith of Abraham, who is the father of us all* (Romans 4:16).

6. **A Comforting Presence**: Isaac, Abraham's son, heard God speak concerning his posterity. When Rebekah was pregnant with their twins, Jacob and Esau, she inquired of God, and His presence spoke a word of insight and loving encouragement:

> *The LORD appeared to him and said…"I will multiply your descendants…all the nations of the earth shall be blessed…two nations are in your womb; and two peoples will be separated from your body"* (Genesis 26:2, 4:25:23).

7. **A Prospering Presence**: Jacob, Isaac's son, received insight from God regarding the accumulation of wealth (Genesis 30:27-43). He even struggled with an angel during the night until he received a blessing. Jacob would then be known as Israel, which means prevailing prince. All who gathered to the presence of God became known as Israelites.

> *So the man* [Jacob] *became exceedingly prosperous, and had large flocks and female and male servants and camels and donkeys* (Genesis 30:37-38, 43).

> *He said, "Your name shall no longer be Jacob, but Israel; for you have striven with God and with men and have prevailed"* (Genesis 32:28, 30).

8. **A Promoting Presence**: Jacob's son Joseph was visited by God's presence in dreams, so much so that he was known as a dreamer. During his captivity in Egypt, he was able to correctly interpret what God was speaking to others in dreams, even the ruler Pharaoh.

> *Now he had still another dream, and related it to his brothers, and said, "Lo, I have had still another dream;*

Learn From Ancient Experiences

and behold, the sun and the moon and eleven stars were bowing down to me" (Genesis 37:9).

So Pharaoh said to Joseph, "Since God has informed you of all this, there is no one so discerning and wise as you are. You shall be over my house...only in the throne I will be greater than you" (Genesis 41:39-41).

9. **A Delivering Presence**: Moses appears in the 7th generation after Abraham. When he was 80 years old, Moses heard God speak and he responded. He then interacted with the presence of God several times before, during, and after Israel's deliverance from Egypt. During this event God said He would take all who sought to be faithful, to be His people.

Say, therefore, to the sons of Israel, "I am the LORD, and I will bring you out from under the burdens of the Egyptians...I will also redeem you with an outstretched arm and with great judgments. Then I will take you for My people, and I will be your God; and you shall know that I am the LORD your God" (Exodus 6:6-7).

And He said, "My presence shall go with you, and I will give you rest." (Exodus 33:14).

10. **A Visible Presence**: After Israel left Egypt, God spoke to Moses and the whole assembly at Mount Sinai. The people, however, asked God to speak to them only through Moses (Exodus chapters 19-20). God then instructed Moses to build a Tent of Meeting so His presence could dwell among them within a visible covering.

Let them construct a sanctuary...that I may dwell among them (Exodus 25:8).

Then the cloud covered the tent of meeting, and the glory [visible presence] *of the LORD filled the tabernacle* (Exodus 40:34).

11. **A Guiding Presence:** God intended to bring Israel into their Promised Land following a two year journey (Numbers 9:1). The trek was intended to transition their servant attitude into a people who could take possession of His promises. Sadly, they failed to become serious believers, so they spent 40 years transitioning in the wilderness.

And He said, "My presence shall go with you and I will give you rest" (Exodus 33:14).

O God, when You went forth before Your people, when You marched through the wilderness…Sinai itself quaked at the presence of God… (Psalms 68:7-8).

12. **A Victorious Presence:** As Israel entered the Promised Land and took possession of Canaan, God raised up judges to provide victorious leadership. Not only were the judges military leaders, they also provided spiritual insight for the Lord was with them.

When the LORD raised up judges for them, the LORD was with the judge and delivered them from the hand of their enemies (Judges 2:18).

Then Samuel said, "Gather all Israel to Mizpah and I will pray to the Lord for you." They gathered…and said there, "We have sinned against the LORD." And Samuel judged [as an arbitrator] *the sons of Israel at Mizpah* (1 Samuel 7:5-6).

Learn From Ancient Experiences

13. **A Worshipful Presence:** David was born in the 7th generation after Moses. He sang and worshiped God as a young shepherd. When he became king, he proposed a more grandiose representation of God's presence, a temple in Jerusalem. David wrote most of the Psalms in our Bible, giving expression to the wonders and dealings of God.

> *Where can I go from Your Spirit? Or where can I flee from Your presence?* (Psalms 139:7)

> *I will bless the LORD who has counseled me...I have set the LORD continually before me; because He is at my right hand, I will not be shaken* (Psalms 16:7-8).

> *When they praised the LORD...the house of the LORD, was filled with a cloud...for the glory of the LORD filled the house* (2 Chronicles 5:13-14).

Again, this is just a small sampling of the many recorded events in Scripture where the presence of God interacted with His children. Our Bible's Old and New Testament are full of examples that illustrate God's interactive presence. God cares more about each of us and our maturing development than we realize.

From the beginning of human history, God's presence has interacted with those willing to hear and respond to His guidance. The presence of the Eternal I AM is a reality each of us can experience. Without God's revealing presence, we come up short of real maturity. Interacting with His presence, we are indeed very highly favored and blessed!

Imperfect People

It is obvious that written Scripture could not record every time the presence of God came and spoke to people. Nor could it record every time someone responded to God's presence. If those events were all written, the world could not contain all the books.

From the limited references we have cited, we can identify a few of the concerns to which God lends insight. His presence gave Adam and Eve instruction that would have kept them from the deathly extremes of trial and error. His presence instructed Cain about adjusting his attitude. The presence of God instructed Abraham about where to live, about his children, family discord, and taught him to trust His guidance. God's presence interacted with Noah regarding the saving of his family, with Moses about Israel's salvation, and with Joshua about receiving the promise given to Abraham.

It is important to realize these are examples of God's presence coming to ordinary people who had all sorts of imperfections. Each of them, as well as others, had their issues. For example, Noah was, at times, a drunk; Abraham was too old; Isaac was a daydreamer; Jacob was deceitful; Leah was ugly; Joseph was abused; Moses had a low self-image; Gideon was afraid; Samson was a womanizer; Rahab was a prostitute; Jeremiah was too young.

The list goes on: David was an adulterer and murderer; Elijah was suicidal; Jonah ran from God; Naomi was a widow; Peter denied Christ; Martha was a worrier; the Samaritan woman was married five times; Zaccheus was too small; Paul was too religious; Timothy had stomach issues; Lazarus died prematurely. What made them noteworthy was their response to the direction given by the presence of God. These were ordinary and flawed people whom God used in extraordinary ways.

These were ordinary and flawed people whom God used in extraordinary ways.

Two reflective questions come to mind: What are your own shortcomings and how has God used you in extraordinary ways? Without acknowledging your weaknesses, you can slow your spiritual growth. Without remembering how God has been with you in the past, you could lose hope!

The Bible's Old Testament accounts of God's interaction with people throughout ancient times illustrate how God does not abandon us in our weaknesses, infirmities, and imperfections. He cares about us and offers insight regarding our bad attitudes, mistaken ideas, flawed work, and harmful thoughts. Why? Because He loves each of us, without qualifications!

Multitudes have written about their experience since the Scriptures were compiled. The number of books giving accounts of people's interaction with God in the twenty-first century alone is almost innumerable.

We do not have to walk this life abandoned to our shortcomings. God desires to share insights that will lead us through and beyond the situations we find ourselves experiencing. We do not want to be like Israel of old and shy away from God's helpful and insightful presence.

Know God and His Ways

Despite the accounts in Scripture and the subsequent books that have been written, many still wonder if anyone can really know God or understand His ways. Most of us have heard and many can even quote, the two verses in Scripture that appear to tell us the thoughts and ways of God are beyond our ability to comprehend.

> *"For My thoughts are not your thoughts, nor are your ways My ways," declares the LORD. "For as the heavens are higher than the earth, so are My ways higher than your ways and My thoughts than your thoughts"* (Isaiah 55:8-9).

> *Oh, the depth of the riches both of the wisdom and knowledge of God! How unsearchable are His judgments and unfathomable His ways* (Romans 11:33).

The problem with using these verses to indicate we cannot know God or enter heavenly levels of understanding is that they are taken out of context. In context, they do not say what we have been led to believe.

The Isaiah passage is making a truthful statement regarding unrepentant people. An unrepentant attitude does make God's thoughts and ways, like the Tree of Life, beyond our ability to receive. Our repentance changes everything.

> *Incline your ear and come to Me. Listen, that you may live…Seek the LORD…call upon Him while He is near.*

Learn From Ancient Experiences

Let the wicked forsake his way and the unrighteous man his thoughts; and let him return to the LORD, and He will have compassion on him...for He will abundantly pardon (Isaiah 55:3, 6).

In the Romans verse, Paul is not saying we can't go deeper into the things of God. He is saying we should not settle for what we already know or our current level of understanding. Let's go deeper! There is no end to what we can learn of the Eternal I Am, and there should be no end to our growing appreciation of Him.

Will we stand on the question, "Who can hear God and live?" as though He is beyond ordinary peoples capacity to hear and receive? The first step is to acknowledge He "IS," and as our loving Father, His desire is for our wellbeing. Then we can begin to hear, receive, and even interact with His presence.

Sometimes we take things at face value and don't consider the intricacies involved. Take a rock, for example. We can observe it's heavy, it's solid, and it's rough. But if we were to look deeper, we would see that the rock is composed of silicon and other elements. What about the silicon? If we looked deeper into the silicon, we might see that it is made up of atoms, which in turn are composed of protons, neutrons, and electrons. And these protons in turn...well, I'll stop there. That simple rock is not so simple after all!

Like the rock, the richness that God has built into our life experience on the earth has many layers that can be examined and experienced. What level of awareness is sufficient for you? How deep will we look into the rich vastness of the Eternal I Am?

These are the things God has revealed to us by his Spirit. The Spirit searches all things, even the deep things of God (1 Corinthians 2:10).

Scripture has much more to say about the ways of God than is contained in the few verses we have quoted. We are told ten times in Scripture that God wants "to teach" us His ways and eight times we "can know" His ways. Scripture also says we "can keep" the ways of God (five times) and "walk in" His ways (twenty times).

Why do we focus on two passages that, out of context, indicate God's ways are beyond us and ignore the forty-three references that say they are not beyond our understanding? Jesus gave us insightful clarity about how to go beyond our "not knowing" when He said:

> *Ask and it will be given to you; seek, and you will find; knock and it will be opened to you. For everyone who asks receives, and he who seeks finds, and to him who knocks it will be opened* (Matthew 7:7-8).

God's ways are the relational tools that work into us the eternal qualities of His own heart. We elaborate in detail on the primary ways of God in my book, *The Christ Culture*. God's ways are the methods and processes He uses to help us grow and mature into what He created us to be. God's ways work into us the eternal qualities of His own nature. As His ways become our ways, our lives become more fruitful. Embracing the presence of God and His ways among us are vital to our maturing growth.

Scripture continually reminds us of God's desire to be our primary guiding light. From the beginning of recorded history in the book of Genesis through the last book of the Bible, God offers each of us a personal relationship with His insightful presence. We do not have to limit ourselves to learning by trial and error or the extremes of good and evil.

God and His ways are not hidden to those who seek to know, understand, and walk in them. Why should anyone be satisfied with only knowing God exists or simply calling on Him to help during emergencies? Let us prayerfully pursue His wise counsel.

God and His ways are not hidden to those who seek to know.

Just as the Holy Spirit says, "Today if you hear His voice…" (Hebrews 3:7).

It is written in the prophets, "And they shall all be taught of God." Everyone who has heard and learned from the Father… (John 6:45).

Our pursuit of the heart of God deepens our relationship with Him and also impacts our relationship with each other. When we better understand God's intentions and respond to His inspiring presence in our midst, we receive revealing insight and our daily lives are improved.

While Scripture can be a facilitator, there is no better way to learn of God than through personal interaction with Him. Our interaction helps us mature into human expressions of

His image and likeness; becoming better reflections and resemblances of His heart.

Memorize: *Ask and it will be given to you; seek, and you will find; knock and it will be opened to you. For everyone who asks receives, and he who seeks finds, and to him who knocks it will be opened* (Matthew 7:7-8).

Questions for reflection:

1. How are each of us equipped to interact with God and the spiritual realm?

2. Were these "heroes of the faith" really the best of the best?"

3. Why does the Eternal I Am interact with such imperfect people?

Chapter 5

Our Living Example

As I have noted, during my early life our family moved across the country visiting different ministries. It was our way of life as we sought to understand more about God and His ways among us. There were times we stayed in a location for just a few weeks and other times for several months.

We wanted to hear what was being taught and observe how God was moving in others' personal lives and ministries. This was before the internet became a simpler way to visit, hear, and readily observe as it is today. Along the way, I had the opportunity to converse with many people, some in nationally recognized ministries.

As we moved from place to place, I received valuable insight by instruction, reading, prayer, and through much observation. One day I sensed God say to me that it was time to stop traveling so what I was perceiving and learning could "drop a foot" from my head into my heart, from understandings into relational experiences.

At the time, we were in Dallas, Texas. So I stopped traveling and became part of a local fellowship of believers who highly valued Scripture, fellowship, and times of worship. My experience with them included many inspiring discussions about Scripture and the ways of God. As I experienced the love and care of God that was manifested in their lives, my understanding of God and His ways were enhanced.

Today, for many, the internet has become a primary source for obtaining insight. If you have internet access, you can find out something about nearly every conceivable topic. A Google search of the word "truth" returns over 700 million results. There are unlimited sources of information available, no further away than the click of a button.

Yes, the availability of knowledge has certainly increased. I was blessed in my earlier years to learn directly from people who had a wealth of personal experience. Then the time came for me to go beyond obtaining knowledge to experiencing for myself the relational power of the truths God was sharing with me.

The Predicted One

There will be no end to the increase of His government or of peace…to establish it and to uphold it with justice and righteousness from then on and forevermore (Isaiah 9:7).

And likewise, all the prophets who have spoken, from Samuel and his successors onward, also announced these days (Acts 3:24).

Our Living Example

The era of the New Testament begins with the birth of this promised one. The forecasted event was announced, in that day, in a variety of ways—angels proclaimed it, heavenly hosts were heard singing of it, and a sign appeared in the stars of heaven:

An angel of the Lord appeared to him in a dream, saying, "Behold, the virgin shall be with child and shall bear a Son, and they shall call His name Immanuel," which translated means, "God with us" (Matthew 1:20-23).

The angel Gabriel was sent from God...And Mary said to the angel, "How can this be, since I am a virgin?" The angel answered and said to her, "The Holy Spirit will come upon you, and the power of the Most High will overshadow you; and...the holy Child shall be called the Son of God" (Luke 1:26, 34-37).

The angel said to them [shepherds in the field], *"Do not be afraid; for behold I bring you good news of great joy which will be for all the people; for today... there has been born for you a Savior, who is Christ the Lord...there appeared with the angel a multitude of the heavenly host praising God"* (Luke 2:10-11, 13).

"Where is He who has been born King...for we [the Magi] *saw His star in the east and have come to worship Him"* (Matthew 2:2, 11).

When the appointed time arrived, God spoke and His expression entered the womb of a virgin woman. The deposit of God's expressive voice submitted to the creative and forming process that happens when a child is formed in a mother's womb. Placement and growth in the womb allowed this unique deposit of God to experience the physical processes and emotional swings of a human pregnancy. How can we know this? According to healthline.com,

> The fetus's middle ear typically develops at week 20, and with this development your baby can hear your heartbeat and voice…The baby's lungs are not fully developed in the early stages of the third trimester [25 weeks], but it may weigh about 4 pounds and is able to recognize changes in sound. The baby is surrounded by darkness, but it can detect bright lights from outside the womb.

Today, science can demonstrate that a child in the womb responds to the sounds that are within the mother's reach, the melody of music, the harsh or encouraging words that are said, as well as the emotional swings that a mother experiences. It has also been shown that what a mother experiences during pregnancy (food, drink, and drugs consumed, and good and bad emotions) has positive and negative effects on the developing child as well.

Logos Becomes a Son

When the Eternal I Am voiced His intention over two thousand years ago, His life-giving expressive action entered the womb of Mary. This unique child was to be called Jesus Christ, which means "Jesus the anointed" or "the anointed Jesus."

> *And the Word* [logos] *became flesh, and dwelt among us, and we saw His glory, glory as of the only begotten from the Father* (John 1:14).

Our Living Example

Our New Testament translates two Greek words logos and rhema (among others) into English as "word." Both Greek words have similar meanings, yet they are clearly different. Scripture uses both to speak of dissimilar features of a spoken expression. The difference provides an insight that is hidden by translating both as word in our Bibles.

According to Spiros Zodhiates (*Hebrew-Greek Key Word Study Bible*): "Rhema is a word spoken or uttered, it stands for the subject matter of the spoken word, the thing which is spoken about." Rhema speaks of the content of what was said, which can be received and understood. Here are two examples:

> *"The words* [rhema] *that I have spoken to you are spirit and are life"...Simon Peter answered Him, "Lord, to whom shall we go? You have words* [rhema] *of eternal life"* (John 6:63, 68).

> *This is the third time I am coming to you. Every fact* [rhema] *is to be confirmed by the testimony of two or three witnesses* (2 Corinthians 13:1).

Rhema is the understandable content of a spoken expression. Scripture is a rhema that God has provided through multiple authors over many centuries, for us to read and contemplate, so we can begin to understand. This includes the comments of Jesus and the events recorded in Scripture. Our written Scripture is considered God's rhema.

The Greek word *logos* has a different meaning. It is defined by Zodhiates as: "intelligence, a word that is the expression of intelligence...sound, noise, or utterance." Logos is the action of speaking and refers to the expressive emotional force and energetic action that proceeds from an originator.

Logos conveys the feelings and heartfelt intent of the one speaking while rhema refers to the content of what was actually said. When God speaks, His voice is infused with His loving attitude, tone, and emotion. Logos is the expressive action while rhema is the actual words. Some people over the years have referred to God's heart expression as the "Spirit of the word" (logos of the rhema).

Let's read the following Scripture quotes, substituting the Greek for the English: *Thy logos is alive and active* (Hebrews 4:12); *Thy logos formed the heavens and earth* (2 Peter 3:5); *Thy logos shall not pass away* (Matthew 24:35); and, *Thy logos is truth* (John 17:17).

Logos is the expressive action of the Spirit of God that came into the womb of Mary, to be formed into the man Jesus, and to live as a human son of God. Scripture says Jesus was the only human uniquely begotten in this manner. In contrast, the first Adam's spirit was infused into a formed body. The rest of us receive our spirit of life from our parents.

The Voice Gives Life

Translating logos into "word" masks the subtle, yet crucial difference between the written Scripture we read and the life-giving voice of God that we hear. Reading and repeating the written word (rhema) can facilitate our openness to receive what God desires to say to our hearts. However, it is the voice (logos) of His Spirit that gives the written word relevancy.

Our Living Example

The Eternal I Am uses a variety of messengers to deliver His message. Occasionally, angelic messengers spoke as though they were God himself (Genesis 22:11-12). Jesus, however, was more than a messenger; he is the spoken expression (logos) that uniquely became a visible flesh and blood human, to deliver the understandable message (rhema) of God. The articulated words of Jesus convey God's heart, mind, will, and desire for our lives.

Logos is the life-giving expressive voice of God, the truth that is alive, active, and will not pass away. The voice of God carries more than a word; it is infused with attitude, tone, and emotion. The life that is resident in Scripture, the written word, is dependent more on the voice or manner in which the words are expressed than in the words themselves. Were the words God spoke and are recorded in Scripture infused with the tone and emotion of a loving Father or as demanding commands?

The Bible shares the articulated thoughts and words of God that were spoken and recorded by people of old. A verse or written portion, however, may not clearly convey God's attitude, emotional emphasis, or full intention. So we can ask, are His words (rhema) expressed (logos) as harsh commands or as loving enticements? Are they intended as guides to our steps or as decrees of law? Without hearing His expressive voice, who knows for sure? I suspect God's words are generally spoken as enticing invitations.

When we are open to God's insightful thoughts, we can sense and hear His voice speak to us. This is when they become living words. As God quickens a word or thought to our consciousness, His will can be felt, perceived, heard, and known. Without the quickening Spirit of God, the written word can be lifeless, even deadly.

> *Such confidence we have through Christ toward God...not of the letter but of the Spirit; for the letter kills, but the Spirit gives life* (2 Corinthians 3:4-6).

This is another good reason why we want to know and experience God beyond the written word of Scripture. When the written word is quickened by God's Spirit, it is alive and comes to us as a fresh expression for our specific moment and situation. When God speaks a word to us, His heart's emotional intent is included.

For centuries, we have been encouraged to "get into the Word." Reading Scripture can facilitate our understanding and many times provide a focus that opens our consciousness up to the voice of God. Scripture, without the quickening of the Spirit of God upon our spirit, can be misunderstood. I want to encourage you, on a daily basis, to be open to the inclinations of God's voice. The written is important but the spoken, what God says to your own consciousness, is more valuable and life-giving.

A Son of Man and God

Jesus lived a natural life with all its growth and learning processes. He lived as a human son of God by doing and saying what he saw and heard his heavenly Father say and do. He was a living reflection and resemblance of our Father's character, attitude, and personality (CAP). Jesus was, as we are created to be, a son of man and a son of God.

Our Living Example

Jesus was, as we are created to be, a son of man and a son of God.

Jesus demonstrated how we, as children (sons and daughters) of God, are to seek and respond to the Father's guiding presence throughout our lifetime. He responded as a son to his earthly parents during childhood and to his heavenly Father as an adult.

The Child continued to grow and become strong, increasing in wisdom; and the grace of God was upon Him (Luke 2:40).

> *He had to be made like His brethren in all things, so that He might become a merciful and faithful high priest in things pertaining to God...For since He Himself was tempted in that which He has suffered, He is able to come to the aid of those who are tempted* (Hebrews 2:17-18).

As a son of humanity, Jesus demonstrated how we are to live as both natural and spiritual people. He always referred to himself as the son of man and spoke of God as his Father. As a son, Jesus so exactly reflected and resembled the heart of God that he was recognized as the firstborn of the many that would follow his example.

> *...so that He would be the firstborn among many brethren* (Romans 8:29).

As a son of God, Jesus demonstrated how God can be our insightful guide through life. Instead of just following the Laws of God, Jesus entertained the presence of his Father and sought direction for his life, day by day, from childhood to death:

> *Jesus answered, "Truly, truly, I say to you, the Son can do nothing of Himself, unless it is something He sees the Father doing; for whatever the Father does, these things the Son also does in like manner"* (John 5:19).

> *Then Jesus...fell on His face and prayed, saying, "My Father, if it is possible, let this cup pass from Me; yet not as I will, but as You will"* (Mathew 26:36-39).

Jesus went through the same temptations we experience (Hebrews 5:8). This could only happen if he was truly a human and his access to the eternal insight and divine power of God was similar to ours. As a son, Jesus did not know everything. He did, however, walk in close communion with his heavenly Father, who revealed what was needed at the time. We have the same access to the guiding insights of God's presence.

For us to obediently respond to God's voice, we must be able to hear Him. Whether you realize it or not, we all have an inner ear; it's one of our spiritual senses. Our inner spiritual ear enables each of us to hear and receive what God speaks. Yes, everyone can hear and relate to the Eternal One! Quite often we hear and do not realize what we are experiencing. God may be sharing insight with you.

You might ask, "That's all well and good, Keith, but how can I know if I'm really hearing the voice of God?" First, you need to acknowledge that God can speak to you; and second, that He will speak to you. Of course, the big question on everyone's mind is, "How can I know He is the one who is speaking and it's not just my own thoughts. I never hear an audible voice." Many books have been written on this one subject alone, but I'll try to put it as simply as I can. Jesus said: "My sheep hear My voice, and I know them, and they follow Me" (John 10:27). When we know we are His children and belong to Him, we can learn to discern His voice!

The Eternal One is our Father. Jesus was God's ultimate "show and tell" example for all humanity, demonstrating our Father's design for each of us as His children. Scripture records what appears to be God's first mention of humankind when He said:

> *"Let Us make man* [kind] *in Our image, according to Our likeness"* (Genesis 2:26).

The Hebrew words "image" and "likeness" in the above verse can be accurately translated as "reflection" and "resemblance." These words more appropriately reflect the original Hebrew. We are intended to become reflections that resemble our multifaceted Father.

Reflection refers to the action of a mirror, which reflects what is being viewed. We are designed to reflect God so others can comprehend Him when they observe us. When we properly reflect the character, attitude, and personality (CAP) of God's heart, it can appear as though He is in us. Realistically we are as mirrors that reflect Him. All glory for who we are and what we do really belongs to God.

> *But we all, with unveiled face, beholding as in a mirror the glory of the Lord, are being transformed into the same image* [and likeness] *from glory to glory, just as from the Lord, the Spirit* (2 Corinthians 3:18).

Resemblance however, refers to the similarity of a child to a parent. We are birthed into this life to resemble God as children, who grow to resemble His heart character, attitude and personality (CAP). God is our Father, our originating and sustaining source. When we resemble His heart, others can comprehend Him in our CAP as well as our actions.

> *Until we all attain to the unity of the faith, and of the knowledge of the Son of God, to a mature man, to the measure of the stature which belongs to the fullness of Christ* (Ephesians 4:13).

> *Therefore be imitators of God, as beloved children; and walk in love, just as Christ also loved you and gave Himself up for us, an offering and a sacrifice to God as a fragrant aroma* (Ephesians 5:1-2).

God sent His expressive voice into the earth as Jesus Christ, to deal with the sin issue (Hebrews 9:28). Scripture teaches us that sin is not just our erroneous actions—it is the condition of our heart when we live isolated from His guiding presence (Romans 1:20-21). Sin is what we think and do apart or separated from God. Ignoring His insightful presence tends to keep us in our sinful separation.

> *…whatever is not from faith is sin* (Romans 14:22-23).

When disciplining a child, it's all too easy for a parent to succumb to requiring outward compliance. For example, when two siblings get into a fight and the parent intervenes, does the parent settle for a meaningless "I'm sorry" from each of the offenders, or is an effort made to address the motivational issues?

An Unnoticed

With the coming of Jesus, God addressed more than the fact that we are flawed people in need of His saving grace. God wanted to show us and teach us how to respond to His guiding influence as children. This is how we become one with Him and His purpose for our lives. Note the relational value in the following verses:

> *The LORD has today declared you to be His people, a treasured possession* (Deuteronomy 26:18).

> *For you have not received a spirit of slavery leading to fear again, but you have received a spirit of adoption as sons by which we cry out, "Abba! Father!"* (Romans 8:15)

> *Because you are sons, God has sent forth the Spirit of His Son into our hearts, crying, "Abba! Father!"* (Galatians 4:6)

God wants us to realize we can have a child-to-Father fellowship with Him. It is the spirit of life in each living person that gives us an ingrained ability to communicate with our heavenly Father. It is our fellowship with the presence of He Who Is that reveals God's heart and draws us into better reflections and resemblances of our Father. Jesus prayed:

> *Holy Father, keep them in Your name...that they may be one even as We are...that they may all be one; even as You, Father, are in Me and I in You, that they also may be in Us* (John 17:11, 18, 21).

As a son, Jesus did the will of his Father and thus was one with God. I like to refer to this interactive oneness as the culture of Christ. This type of agreeing interaction with God is the heart of Christianity. Our fellowship with His presence makes Christianity more of a faith than a religion. The influence of Christ among us is how God transforms us into fuller expressions of His CAP. (See *The Christ Culture,* Chapter 4)

Our fellowship with His presence makes Christianity more of a faith than a religion.

Jesus declared he would never leave or forsake us and would always be with us. He, as the presence of God with us, said he would be "in the midst" of our godly interactions.

> *He Himself has said, "I will never desert you, nor will I ever forsake you," so that we confidently say, "The Lord is my helper…"* (Hebrews 13:5-6).

> *For where two or three have gathered together in My name, I am there in their midst* (Matthew 18:20).

> *And lo, I am with you always, even to the end of the age* (Matthew 28:20).

As well as instructing us in the Lord's Prayer, to pray to God as our Father, Jesus instructed the disciples at the end of his time as a human, to pray to our heavenly Father in his name.

Our Living Example

In that day you will ask in My name, and I do not say to you that I will request of the Father on your behalf; for the Father Himself loves you (John 16:26).

This involves more than saying "in the name of Jesus." The name speaks of us identifying with Jesus as responsive children of God. We are to ask God as people who are developing into the character, attitude, and personality (CAP) of Jesus and walking in union with God as he did.

Jesus, to a large degree, was restricted to the limitations of natural life, yet he lived a natural life as a spiritual person by staying in close fellowship with God. Jesus illustrated how we can simultaneously live this life as both natural and spiritual people at the same time.

The Gospel of John declared the spoken expression of God's Spirit is the light of our human life.

All things came into being through Him, and apart from Him nothing came into being that has come into being. In Him was life, and the life was the Light of men (John 1:3-4).

The expressive voice of God came to live as Jesus Christ, to reveal God's desire to be the light of every life. The life Jesus lived conveys this reality and demonstrates how it works. The Gospel of Matthew adds definition to this understanding of Jesus as a son of the Holy Spirit by saying Jesus would be known by two specific names, "Christ" and "Emmanuel."

Mary, by whom Jesus was born, who is called Christ...Now the birth of Jesus Christ was as follows: when His mother Mary had been betrothed to Joseph, be-

fore they came together she was found to be with child by the Holy Spirit (Matthew 1:16, 18).

Behold, the virgin shall be with child and shall bear a Son, and they shall call His name "Immanuel," which translated means, "God with us" (Matthew 1:23).

The word Christ is translated from the Greek Christos, which means "anointed, anointing" while Emmanuel means "God with us." Putting these two names together is very enlightening. Jesus is literally the expression of God that visually illustrates for us the "anointing of God with us." Jesus demonstrated God's desire to be recognized as the Light of our life, the presence of God that is with us, among us, and in our midst.

This is the same redeeming message God declared from humanity's beginning in the Garden of Eden. It's the message given to Israel at Mount Sinai after God delivered them from captivity. God also desires to be the primary guiding presence in our life process.

Thanks for staying with me this far. I encourage you to continue on. In the next chapter, I'll dig deeper into the nature and mission of Jesus Christ. You may find a few surprises!

Our Living Example

Memorize: *There will be no end to the increase of His government or of peace...to establish it and to uphold it with justice and righteousness from then on and forevermore* (Isaiah 9:7).

Questions for reflection:

1. How did the prophesied "anointed one" come?

2. Was the life of Jesus on the earth anything like our life?

3. How did Jesus know what God wanted him to say and do?

Chapter 6

The Spirit of Truth Reveals

Early in life I observed that God seems to reveal to the current generation insights that are a bit beyond what previous generations embraced. This principle has been especially true for each generation since the Reformation began 500 years ago. We are still coming out and moving away from some of the erroneous concepts and restricting ideas forced on believers by the religious systems of the past.

I've tried to maintain a certain level of openness over the years regarding what I believe so I could consider the fresh insight God may be sharing. Early in life, when I read Scripture, I would begin by asking God to show me what I had not yet seen, which has kept my theology in a state of developing flux.

Consequently, when I consider a new thought or different teaching, I try to look beyond some of the extremes that may be involved and see if there are any connecting core values that would improve or add to my overall understanding of what God "is" saying and doing. There were and still are times when I dismiss or adjust previous understandings as I embrace fresh insight.

I continue to seek, knock, and ask to know and understand all our heavenly Father desires to reveal. I want my concept of the Eternal One and appreciation of the love He has for us to continue to grow and be enhanced!

Natural and Spiritual Man

The spirit is given to us via the initial deposit of God's Spirit in the first Adam. Eve received it from Adam, and we receive our portion of God's Spirit, the spirit of life, from our parents. The incarnation of Jesus Christ over two thousand years ago was a unique event in human history.

The spirit in Jesus came directly into Mary's womb from God's spoken expression. God spoke and His voice was infused into the womb to be formed into a human son. Jesus was the only one that was uniquely born in this manner.

The first 30 years of the life of Jesus was a growing, developing process as a child of man and a child of God, much like you and me. He grew and developed through the things he experienced in family life as a child of Joseph and Mary. What he reasoned, felt, and came to believe aligned with his earthly parents and his heavenly Father. Early in life he learned to communicate with the presence of God. This interaction taught him to reflect and resemble his heavenly Father's character, attitude, and personality (CAP) as a son of God.

When Jesus reached thirty years of age, he entered public ministry to become a visible illustration of "God with us" (Emmanuel). His own testimony confirmed that his words and actions followed the direction God provided.

> *With many such parables He was speaking the word to them, so far as they were able to hear it; and He did not speak to them without a parable; but He was explaining everything privately to His own disciples* (Mark 4:33-34).

God illustrated, in the life of Jesus, a human example of His CAP. As a son, Jesus revealed God's desire for everyone. He was the visual image and likeness of our heavenly Father that we can look to, learn from, and gravitate into resembling.

Jesus always said and did as God directed. Although there were difficult times, like when he asked God if there was any other way, he still responded, "not my will but thine be done" (Luke 22:42). He was a man that did not know everything, but through his daily fellowship with God, discerned God's direction for his life and followed God's lead. Jesus was clearly much more than a good man or a prophet. Jesus was the "pattern son" for each of us.

Two Gospels record the water and Spirit baptisms of Jesus. During the water event, the Spirit of God descended upon him like a dove (Matthew 3:16-17). As a result of the Spirit coming upon him, Jesus was immersed in God's Spirit and was led by the Spirit into a wilderness, to be tempted (Matthew 3:16-4:1; Like 4:1). Since God cannot be tempted (James 1:13), it is obvious that Jesus was a man who followed the lead of his heavenly Father.

As a child of man, Jesus became the firstborn and elder brother of the many believers that would follow his lead (Romans 8:29). As the mature son, Jesus became the author and captain of our salvation, championing the way for us to follow (Hebrews 2:10). As the glorified son, he became the reconciling mediator between God and mankind (1 Timothy 2:5). He is also celebrated as the King of Kings and Lord of Lords.

The life of Jesus, as a son of man, provided a human demonstration of the image and likeness of God that we are created to become. In Jesus, God showed us what the CAP of God looks like in sons and daughters of God. Jesus was and is our pattern, the pattern we are to follow. At the end of his life on earth, Jesus declared:

I am the way, the truth, and the life (John 14:6).

Jesus said, "I am the truthful way to live."

The phrasing in this verse, as some linguists have confirmed, can be translated as: "I am the truthful way to live." Jesus illustrated in a visible way, our Father's desire for all of His human offspring. God desires that each of us become disciplined children that are maturing through life into reflective resemblances of the CAP Jesus demonstrated.

A Temporary State

Jesus walked and talked with his disciples for three years, yet they were not able to comprehend much of the insights he desired to share with them. After three years of teaching and living among them, Jesus said to the disciples:

> "I have many more things to say...but you cannot bear them now" (John 16:12).

The disciples gained insight from Jesus, but as the Israelites in the wilderness and many of us today, they were still held captive by many of the comprehensions and understandings we have been taught. They needed something more than the spoken words of Jesus to bring them out of their captive perceptions and into the clarity of God's desire for their life.

A jolt to their understanding was about to come and it would release them into the perceptions and life experiences that they were unable to see while Jesus was with them as a man. Just before his death, Jesus voiced an insightful statement and then confirmed it with a prayer:

> "I came forth from the Father and have come into the world; I am leaving the world again and going to the Father" (John 16:28).

> He said, "Father, the hour has come; glorify Thy Son, that the Son may glorify Thee...And now, glorify Thou Me together with Thyself, Father, with the glory which I had with Thee before the world was" (John 17:1, 5).

At this juncture, Jesus informed his disciples that he was about to return to his former glory as the spoken expression

The Spirit of Truth Reveals

of God. The Spirit in Jesus would return to His pre-human existence as God's voice. He would leave the natural form and function beyond the humanity that restricted him to a single time frame and earthly location, to glorify God in multiple manifestations and visitations. The Spirit of Jesus would again function as the expressive voice of the Eternal I Am.

The arrest, conviction, crucifixion, and death of Jesus was unexpected. It shocked their perception of the Messiah's reign and crushed their immediate expectations for a better life. Their understanding of God's kingdom was about to change.

This was a time of transition that would bring new clarity to the purpose, life, and teaching of Jesus. Keep in mind the fact that Jesus was trying to explain spiritual perceptions and realities to followers that were still very earthly minded. They expected to crown Jesus King, remove their overlords, and forcibly take the world; much like the Israelites did when they forcibly entered Canaan.

Although Jesus knew his going and coming was beyond the disciples ability to clearly comprehend; during the last supper he ate with them and took time to describe the change that was about to happen.

In Chapters 14 through 17 of John's Gospel, Jesus spoke of God and emphasized: God is his source and his pre-human existence was as the voice of God. He was leaving this natural state of existence so he could return and more effectively encourage people into the fellowship of God's presence, as the Holy Spirit of Truth.

> *In that day you will know that I am in My Father, and you in Me, and I in you...We* [same Spirit] *will*

come...If anyone loves Me...We will come to him (John 14:20-23).

In John 14, Jesus said he, as a son of man, and our Father were in total agreement, as one (v. 1-3, 9-11, 24), and we are to find this same agreement with God (v. 20, 23, 12). He was leaving the natural life (v. 3, 18, 28) and would return to us as baptizer in God's Spirit (v. 28, 21) to be with us continually (v. 16). He would return to introduce us to God's "immersing presence" (v. 17, 23, 2), to lead and guide us into fuller truth (v. 26). Jesus invites us into the same relational fellowship with God that he experienced during his earthly life (v. 3, 23).

John 15 continues as Jesus amplifies the reasons for Spirit baptisms are to "anoint" and "enlighten" us. We are invited to know God and become one with the Spirit of our Father and His son Jesus. When we are in agreement and properly joined, we become the body of Christ in the earth.

This fresh revealing would be as an anointing and enlightening presence of the Spirit of the Father and son, the same Spirit in two different revealings. Jesus spoke of being our helper, comforter, and revealer of truth. He was to return as God's baptizing Spirit, to not only abide with us but to progressively guide believers into the fuller perceptions and realizations of spiritual life they were unable to receive from his natural presence.

Jesus would no longer be restrained by the laws of the natural realm. The disciples' inclination toward believing only what their natural eye could observe was about to change. They were going to learn God's presence can be with us as an enlightening and enabling force.

Transitional Times

Transition is an important part of any beginning. Without transition, beginnings are rarely established. We generally require some time to grasp what is becoming a new reality. While we accept and process into the new reality, we also learn to let go of what was our previous perception and let the past fade away.

The crucifixion of Jesus came on the very day the Passover was celebrated. The first Passover happened 1500 years earlier as a preparation for the Exodus from Egyptian captivity. The children of Jacob and a huge mixed multitude made a commitment to the God of Abraham by slaying a sacrificial lamb, applying the blood to the doorpost of their dwellings, and consuming its flesh so the lamb became an absorbed part of them.

The first Passover spared lives from death and began a process that resulted in a release from their captors. People were instructed to apply the lamb's blood to their dwellings and then eat the lamb. They were to be fully clothed and ready for travel for this was a new beginning. Their life was changing. They entered a time of transition.

Their full release from captivity, however, required two different transitional times. The first was experienced as they traveled out of Egypt and through the Red Sea where they observed the destruction of Egypt's pursuing army. They were now physically free people.

Fifty days after the Passover they celebrated their freedom in the first Pentecost, a festival of light. They were free from their servitude to Egypt, which symbolizes the world. What a fitting celebration!

While Israel's physical deliverance was complete, there was another transition ahead. This time of adjustment was to free their soul from previous perceptions and bring their beliefs about life into alignment with God's purposes. They needed mental and emotional release from the servant mindset that kept them dependent on overlords for basic needs—food and housing. Servants did not earn wages or own land. They needed to become a productive and self-supporting people.

The wilderness journey from Egypt to Canaan was to bring about a change in their perception of life. God even instructed Moses to go the long way rather than take the shortest route, lest they shrink from the job that was ahead of them (Exodus 13:17). As God shared His perspectives, they were given time to accept and adapt to His view of life. During this time they were to root out, put off, and dismiss the perceptions they learned as captives.

During this transition, God showered on them many examples of His ability to provide without overlords. He provided food and water, health and healing from disease, clothing that did not wear out, and victory in battle. God even verified that His presence would be with them through their process:

> *He said, "My presence shall go with you, and I will give you rest"* (Exodus 33:14).

The Israelites' full release from the effects of their captivity in Egypt became a lifelong process. This Old Testament example illustrates how our full salvation can be a lifelong process of adapting God's ways, while we root out the enslaving ways of this world. We are today, as Israel was then, still struggling with our worldly perceptions and God's purpose for our life.

Our full salvation can be a lifelong process
of adapting God's ways.

Does it bother you when I say that salvation is an ongoing process (not a one-time event)? Let me ask you a simple question: If God left you the way you were when He came into your life, or with the few adjustments you immediately experienced, how would that reflect on His saving purpose? There was a common saying among believers in the 1960s, "Please be patient, God is not finished with me yet." Can you relate?

Two Little Whiles

The end of the earthly life of Jesus took place on that year's Passover, when the sacrificial lamb was slain. His crucifixion began the fifty-day transitional time between Passover and Pentecost. The followers of Jesus would begin a transitional process of grasping what was coming and letting go of many of their previous perceptions.

Before the crucifixion Jesus made a comment that is generally overlooked.

> *"Are you deliberating together about this, that I said, 'A little while, and you will not see Me, and again a little while, and you will see Me'? Truly, truly, I say...you will grieve, but your grief will be turned into joy...your heart will rejoice, and no one will take your joy away from you"* (John 16:19-22).

In this comment, Jesus said there would be "two" little whiles regarding their ability to see him. The word "again" separates the two. He was to leave them in a little while, and they would not be able to see him. Then after a second little while, they would see him.

The death of Jesus at Passover activated the first "little while." For three days he was removed from their sight, and they grieved because he was no longer with them.

When the body of Jesus was raised from the dead (inactive earthly state), he appeared to people as a Spirit Being. These appearances demonstrated Jesus was not really dead but alive. They needed to see his physical resemblance in order to realize it was really Jesus. This began their process of visualizing Jesus as a Spirit, much more than an anointed man. Their grief began to find relief but a lack of understanding during this time of transition kept them from full relief and lasting joy.

As Jesus appeared to followers in a human-like form, they began to see him as a Spirit that was not physical yet could be sensed—seen, felt, and touched. They began to see the Jesus that walked with them was no longer limited to time and space movements or appearances. Seeing Jesus this way, with their natural eyes, prepared them for his return as the baptizing and anointing presence of God's Holy Spirit.

The visual appearing between the two "little whiles" was a temporary situation. His glorified body was not intended to be an ongoing realization. Jesus said to her:

"Stop clinging to Me [as a human], *for I have not yet as-*

cended to the Father...I ascend to My Father and your Father, and My God and your God" (John 20:17).

The appearances between the resurrection and ascension of Jesus began to reform their perceptions of Jesus, from an anointed physical presence that walked with them, into a Spirit presence. His return would facilitate our daily fellowship with the presence of God.

Today, as with Israel of old, we are still learning how to let the will and ways of God dominate the way we think. It is often a difficult process to let go of previous perceptions and become spiritually minded people. Even after receiving the visible Jesus as our life example, we are all still "working out" our salvation (Philippians 2:12). This is a lifelong process.

The second "little while" was activated when the temporary existence of Jesus ascended out of natural sight. Again, they were not able to see him. A few days later the followers of Jesus began to receive the Father's promise of being clothed with spiritual life.

> *And behold, I am sending forth the promise of My Father upon you; but you are to stay in the city until you are clothed with power from on high* (Luke 24:49).

Before Jesus ascended, he announced: "And lo, I am with you always, even to the end of the age" (Matthew 28:20). How would this be? The Spirit of Jesus was to return as God's anointing, empowering, and enlightening presence. The Spirit of Jesus would never be absent from believers and would seek to lead and guide the willing into the ways of God. Paul repeated the statement of Jesus:

> *For He Himself has said, "I will never desert you, nor will I ever forsake you," so that we confidently say, "The lord is my helper, I will not be afraid...Jesus Christ is the same yesterday and today, yes and forever"* (Hebrews 13:5-8).

As Jesus prepared to ascend into the heavens, he gathered and instructed his followers to wait in Jerusalem for the Father's promise. They were approaching the celebration of light—that year's day of Pentecost.

> *He commanded them to not leave Jerusalem, but to wait for what the Father had promised, "Which," He said, "you heard of from Me...you will be baptized with the Holy Spirit not many days from now"* (Acts 1:4-5).

> *As they were gazing intently...while He was departing, behold, two men in white clothing stood beside them. And they also said, "Men of Galilee, why do you stand looking into the sky? This Jesus, who has been taken up from you into heaven* [spiritual realm], *will come in just the same way as you have watched Him go into heaven"* (Acts 1:10-11).

The instructions Jesus gave and the comments of the two messengers during his ascension are tied together, as one immediately follows the other. They were to wait a few more days for the promise of the Father. Jesus said he would return to them as the baptizer in a third revealing of God's presence, to invite people into the spiritual reality they were unable to understand or receive during his time with them in the flesh.

Before his baptism and anointing in God's Holy Spirit, Jesus was a son of humanity and a son of God, a man just like you and me. During his three-year ministry, the anointed person was a visible expression of "God with us." The appearance between the resurrection and ascension was a precursor to prepare them for the coming that followed the second "little while." His reappearance would be as an outpouring of the Spirit of God that would come upon them, clothe them, and provide an unfading joy.

The visible personage was leaving the life of a human so his Spirit could more effectively invite people through the following ages into the fellowship of God's presence. Jesus would "be seen" with spiritual eyes. The world's sight, through natural eyes, would not be able to see him. His presence of Spirit reveals the will of God and anoints the ways of sons and daughters of God.

Ever since that Pentecost, we are to know Jesus Christ as the man who illustrated the actions and attitude of our heavenly Father and as the anointing and enlightening presence of God. This is true for everyone that looks to God, in their own time, from any location around the world and to each one at the same time. There are no limitations! The Apostles Paul and John add touches of clarity:

> *Even though we have known Christ according to the flesh, yet now we know Him in this way no longer* (2 Corinthians 5:16).
>
> *Jesus said, "Blessed are they who did not see, and yet believed"* (John 20:29).

The additional appearing of Christ is for a greater work of forming the Father's CAP, as was illustrated in the anointed

Jesus, in many sons and daughters. The human life of Jesus amplified God's loving kindness and forgiveness. We are to absorb and consume all we can of the slain lamb (visible example) and become better illustrations of the CAP of Jesus Christ.

The spirit of life in Jesus came from the voice of God; the same voice that created the natural realm, which raised the natural body of Jesus from the dead, and comes upon us in Spirit immersions.

The time between the death of the body of Jesus and his ascension was a time of transition. It reoriented their ideas of who Jesus is, so they could "see" him with their spiritual senses as our baptizer in God's Spirit.

Present or To Come

As Jesus returned to the unrestrained function of Spirit, he would, in a real sense, come to us as our baptizer in God's Spirit. In this function, God draws people into an intimate fellowship with His presence so we can learn to agree and become one with Him.

So why are some people "looking" for a physical return of Jesus? There are several Scriptures that appear to indicate a visible return. This can be a good time to examine one element that feeds the notion. Let's consider the New Testament use of the words "coming" and "presence." The primary Greek word for coming is *erchomai* which means: "to come," in contrast with "to go." This Greek word is used over 600 times in Scripture and is most always translated as "come" and "coming."

By comparison, the Greek *parousia* was also translated in our first English Bibles as "coming." It means: a being near; as a presence that is close.

The *King James Version* of the Bible translates parousia 22 times as coming and two times as presence. During the time of King James, "coming" may have had a strong "presence" connotation, to make it an appropriate translation for that day. Today, however, "coming" misleads Scripture's intent and allows for misperceptions to develop.

The Greek and Hebrew scholar Spiros Zodhiates defines parousia as: to be present, to be at hand. In his notes, Zodhiates explains: The sense of "presence" is so plainly shown in the following verse by the contrast with "absence."

> *As you have always obeyed, not as in my presence* [parousia] *only, but now much more in my absence, work out your salvation with fear and trembling* (Philippians 2:12).

Rotherham's Emphasized Bible is a literal translation of the Bible that uses various methods, such as "emphatic idiom" and special diacritical marks, to bring out nuances of the underlying meanings of the Greek, Hebrew, and Aramaic texts. It was produced in 1902 by Joseph Bryant Rotherham, who described his goal as, "placing the reader of the present time in as good a position as that occupied by the reader of the first century for understanding the Apostolic Writings." Rotherham translates parousia only as presence and never as coming.

Parousia speaks of: being near, present, and at hand. This

word gives no indication of a "will be," or a "to be" as though there could be a delay or a future. The most fitting way to translate parousia and maintain its intended meaning is "presence."

The following verses are where parousia is used in Scripture. These verses are often used to refer to a second coming of Jesus Christ, while they actually speak of his presence as the Spirit of God that is within us. To simplify the read, we have changed the word "coming" to "presence":

> *Abide in Him, so that when He appears, we may have confidence and not shrink away from Him in shame at His presence* (1 John 2:28).
>
> *We made known to you the power and presence of our Lord Jesus Christ...we were eyewitnesses of His majesty* (2 Peter 1:16).
>
> *"What will be the sign of Your presence?"...For just as the lightning comes from the east and flashes even to the west, so will the presence of the Son of Man be...For the presence of the Son of Man...so will the presence of the Son of Man be* (Matthew 24:3, 27, 37, 39).
>
> *Therefore be patient, brethren, until the presence of the Lord...strengthen your hearts, for the presence of the Lord is near* (James 5:7-8).
>
> *Mockers will come...saying, "Where is the promise of His presence"...what sort of people ought you to be, in holy conduct and godliness, looking for and hastening the presence of the day of God* (2 Peter 3:3-4, 11-12).
>
> *With regard to the presence of our Lord Jesus Christ and*

our gathering together to Him...Then that lawless one will be revealed...by the appearance of His presence (2 Thessalonians 2:1, 8).

In the presence of our Lord Jesus with all His saints...For this we say to you by the word of the Lord, that we who are alive and remain unto the presence of the Lord...Now may the God of peace Himself sanctify you entirely... without blame unto the presence of our Lord Jesus Christ (1 Thessalonians 3:13; 4:15; 5:23).

Christ the first fruits, after that those who are Christ's in His presence (1 Corinthians 15:23).

While these verses are used to indicate another visual coming of Jesus, they really speak of the anointing presence of God that has already come to believers. His presence with us is not seen with the natural eye but as the insightful and anointing Spirit of Truth.

As the observers looked up into the heavens when the visual Jesus ascended out of sight, they were told that he would return in like manner. Quite often, Scripture refers to the heavens as God's dwelling, which is a spiritual existence that is not restrained by natural limitations (Matthew 5:34, 45, 48). As we "look up to God," we can see and experience his coming to us as a presence of Spirit.

God-in-Christ has come and His presence, as promised, is always with us although sadly, we are not always aware or attentive. We do not want to be like Israel of old, which after their deliverance, refused to accept the fellowship of God's presence (Exodus 20:19).

> As we "look up to God," we can see
> and experience his coming to us
> as a presence of Spirit.

One with Three Expressions

While God comes and reveals Himself to us in a multitude of ways, we primarily relate to Him as the One that is revealed to us in three relational expressions.

1. As heavenly Father, God is the **Abiding Presence** historically called on for intervention. The Eternal I Am is our ever-present help.

2. As Jesus Christ, God is the **Visible Presence** we observe and learn from, our pattern son. This is why Jesus told Philip, "He that has seen me has seen the Father."

3. As Holy Spirit, God is the **Immersing Presence** that draws us into His intimate fellowship.

The Eternal I Am is an ever-present help in our time of need, as our provisional Father. The I Am appeared in history as our example son Jesus Christ. The I Am also comes as a Holy Spirit presence, to anoint believers. In each case, God is our source of greater truth.

The first and second century believers focused on the fact that God was "with them" as an enlightening and empowering presence. This realization upset the world's perceptions of God and of life in general during the first century following the life of Jesus. It was even reported:

These men who have upset the world have come here also (Acts 17:6).

The voice of God is the life giving expression of the eternal I Am that created this natural universe. It is the same expressive voice that was incarnated to live as a son of man, Jesus Christ. After thirty years of maturing growth and three years of anointed ministry, Jesus returned to the Father to again function as the voice of God. This same expressive voice comes to us today, to enlighten and enrich our lives into a newness of life.

The presence of God is available to everyone to help us overcome the world's misguided approach toward life and learn to be better people. God's presence is not far from anyone. It can be felt and heard as a presence of Spirit.

The disciples learned our fellowship with God-in-Christ does not require a scheduled time or a specific location. While God has come in the past and will come in our future, He is not restricted to either. God-in-Christ promises to be with us as an enlightening and empowering presence to whosoever will, in each generation. He comes to us today!

Memorize: *For He Himself has said, "I will never desert you, nor will I ever forsake you," so that we confidently say, "The lord is my helper...Jesus Christ is the same yesterday and today, yes and forever"* (Hebrews 13:5-8).

Questions for reflection:

1. When did Jesus begin to live as an illustration of "God with us"?

2. Jesus spoke of two "little whiles." What were they?

3. Why are followers of Christ able to see him while the world cannot?

Chapter 7

A Thirst For His Presence

A close friend of mine, a pastor, was helping an established church decide how to proceed. The fellowship included about 20 adults and their growing families. The six young men, considered elders, three generations from the founder, were now functioning without the pastor they had known most of their lives. At one particular meeting the discussion turned toward considering someone who recently had begun to attend their fellowship for the pastoral position.

A cautionary thought was raised when someone said the person being considered for the position had not been baptized in the Holy Spirit. My pastor friend then asked, "How many of you have had the baptism experience?" Only one of those in the meeting raised a hand. It was a bit embarrassing simply because they understood the Holy Spirit baptism was a particular experience that came during a specific type of event.

Each of these young men had experienced the immersing and interactive presence of God while in worship, listening to ministry, reading Scripture, during private meditations, times of prayer, and in conversation about the things of God. Without a doubt, each of them had experienced multiple times, the revealing and anointing presence of God. The problem was that their understanding of the baptism needed to be enlarged.

The Baptism in God's Holy Spirit is not a one-time event or experience that comes with just one obvious evidence. As we explain in this chapter, baptisms are immersions in the presence of God where the spirit we are born with is stirred to receive anointing enablement and enlightening insight from God's influencing presence.

Water and Spirit Baptism

According to three of the four Gospels, John the Baptist was the first person in Scripture to speak of baptism, He spoke of two types, saying:

> *I baptized you with water; but He* [Jesus] *will baptize you with the Holy Spirit"* (Matthew 3:11; Mark 1:8; Luke 3:16).

The Greek word used in Scripture for baptism is *bapto*, which means: to cover wholly with a fluid, dip, or immerse. In the days of the New Testament, yarn, cloth and clothing were routinely bapto'd in dye and whitening agents to change or add color. Similarly people were bapto'd in water as a symbolic wash, to demonstrate their commitment to let go of past perceptions and to cease from ungodly activity. Simply put, baptism at the time was an immersion in water.

John baptized in the Jordan River because he patterned his water baptism after Israel's crossing the Jordan 1500 years earlier, when they first entered the Promised Land. As Israel crossed the Jordan River, it symbolized their 40 years of wandering in the desert ended. They crossed as free people, no longer restrained by the unbelief that kept them from entering 38 years earlier, and began the victorious process of conquering and living in the Promised Land.

John was called "the Baptist" because he publicly baptized people in water as a public testimony of their repentant desire to be more godly people. This was a visible act to illustrate their commitment to live better lives. John's water baptism involved three actions: A person would 1) enter the water, 2) become fully immersed, and 3) exit, affected physically, emotionally, and mentally by the event.

We want to remember that baptism is an immersion we experience.

We want to remember that baptism is an immersion we experience, whether it's in water or in God's Spirit. While John baptized in water, Jesus would baptize in God's Spirit. Jesus said baptizing immersions in Spirit would not come while he was still living as the example son of God (Matthew 16:21).

Scripture is silent about Jesus baptizing anyone in Holy Spirit before returning to his previous existence as the voice of God. There was one time between the resurrection and ascension that Jesus encouraged his followers to be receptive of the Holy Spirit.

> *"As the Father has sent Me, I also send you." And when He had said this, He breathed on them and said to them, "Receive the Holy Spirit"* (John 20:21-22).

Jesus left this natural life and went back to the Father of all spirits, to come again to us as our Baptizer in God's Holy Spirit. Jesus returned as God's living voice to them and to us into to introduce them, and us, into the experience of God's presence among us. The day of Pentecost demonstrated the return of Jesus as the Christ, our anointer.

Pentecost Arrives

As the visible Jesus was ascending into the heavenly spirit realm, disappearing from natural sight, he instructed those watching to remain in Jerusalem for the promise. They were to wait for the enlightening and anointing that would equip them to be effective witnesses of the life of Christ and of his presence with them:

> *"Which," He said, "you heard of from Me…you will be baptized with* [immersed in] *the Holy Spirit not many days from now…you will receive power when the Holy Spirit has come upon you; and you shall be My witnesses"* (Acts 1:4-8).

Fifty days after the crucifixion of Jesus at Passover, Pentecost arrived with the promise.

A Thirst for His Presence

> *Suddenly there came from heaven a noise like a violent, rushing wind, and it filled the whole house where they were sitting. And there appeared to them tongues as of fire distributing themselves, and they rested on each one of them* (Acts 2:2-4).

The promised appearing came as a rushing wind, which they felt and heard. Fiery tongues appeared over each one in the room. These physical manifestations caught everyone's attention. Their natural senses were fully engaged and gave witness to the fact that something out of the ordinary was happening.

The presence of the Spirit of God was poured out upon them as an immersing presence that rested, for this dramatic moment, upon them. This presence of God-in-Christ would lead and guide them into the truth they were unable to receive while the physical Jesus walked the earth.

> *He saved us…by the washing of regeneration and renewing by the Holy Spirit, whom He poured out upon us richly through Jesus Christ our Savior* (Titus 3:5-6).

Salvation includes our renewing and regeneration by the Spirit of God. Before that year's Passover and Pentecost events, their understanding and expectation of "God with us" was largely wrapped up in the physical life of Jesus.

During the transitional time between Passover and Pentecost, Jesus appeared to them as a Spirit with the appearance of the man they knew, enabling the natural eye to see him. So God included their natural senses in this initial return as a presence. This graphic experience left no doubt that God-in-

Christ had returned as an anointing and empowering presence of Spirit.

This appearing did not include the visible personage of Jesus, but the voice of God was clearly involved. Tongues of fire are a visual illustration for enlightening words. This spiritual experience showered enlightenment and revelatory insight. Immersions in God's Spirit immediately began to lead them into greater realizations of truth and began to empower their effectiveness as witnesses.

It fully turned their confusion and grief over the death of Jesus into a lasting joy. Jesus was again with them. Their joy spilled over into miraculous expressions as these Galileans began to speak, for the first time, to the gathering crowd in several different languages unknown to themselves.

Now there were Jews living in Jerusalem, devout men from every nation under heaven. And when this sound occurred, the crowd came together, and were bewildered because each one of them was hearing them speak in his own language...saying, "Why, are not all these who are speaking Galileans? And how is it that we each hear them in our own language to which we were born?" (Acts 2:5-8)

During the experience, Peter proclaimed to the crowd that what they were seeing was spoken of by Joel, one of the last Old Testament prophets (Joel 2:28-32):

God says, "That I will pour forth of My Spirit on all mankind...I will in those days pour forth of My Spirit"...and having received from the Father the promise of the Holy Spirit, He poured forth this which you both see and hear (Acts 2:17-18, 33).

This baptism experience was a real game changer for believers. The recipients of this immersion had fiery tongues appear over them, and they spoke in languages they had not learned. That initial outpouring was unique for the appearance of fiery tongues was not reported to happen again.

This Pentecost was one amazing celebration of light. As God-in-Christ poured forth His Spirit upon these followers of Jesus, the Light began to clarify and their lights began to shine like never before. God's Holy Spirit appeared over them and rested upon them. This empowered them to be more effective witnesses of Christ as an anointing presence with and among them.

The experience and message of the day was so miraculous, invitational, and appealing that 3,000 people that day became partakers of the faith. They were also immersed in the same presence of Christ, of God's Holy Spirit:

> *So then, those who had received his word* [logos-expressive voice] *were baptized; and that day there were added about three thousand souls* [persons]...*Everyone kept feeling a sense of awe...praising God and having favor with all the people. And the Lord was adding to their number day by day* (Acts 2:41, 43, 47).

It was almost like the first Passover, when the family of Israel, who had gone into Egypt four generations earlier (Exodus 6:16-20), were joined by over two million people in their Exodus (Exodus 12:37-38). This mixed multitude believed, as Abraham did, in God's promise of a better life under the guidance of God's Spirit.

People found this new clarity regarding God's involvement in life very appealing and multitudes were drawn into its experience. Those who received this new expression of God's logos (heart-felt voice of God) also experienced immediate effects. Response to this call to faith in Christ allowed the presence of God, which was always available to them, to become more of an enabling influence among them.

To know that God is with you as an empowering presence even though you cannot see Him with the natural eye, liberates, encourages, and empowers everyone to interact with each other in more Christ-like ways. Believers who received this anointing presence became world changing expressions of God's love. They reached out to help the sick, oppressed, and downtrodden. This was a welcome change from the restrictive Jewish religious system they were raised in.

The promise of God's presence, as prophesied by Joel is available to all mankind. Each person who responds to God's invitation to partake of an active fellowship with God's Spirit can experience times in His presence and learn to be more Christ-like. How well are we living, proclaiming, and appealing to people today? Are our lives drawing others into the fellowship of God's presence?

We can all agree that Jesus did not physically return on that special day of Pentecost, but he did come. The Eternal I Am, the God they revered as the Creator was now becoming an empowering presence to all who would receive Him.

As a Sponge

There is a factor regarding baptismal immersions in God's

Spirit that is generally overlooked. What does Scripture mean when it says they were "filled" with the Holy Spirit?

> *Suddenly there came from heaven a noise like a violent, rushing wind, and it filled the whole house...And they were all filled with the Holy Spirit* (Acts 2:2, 4).

There are two different Greek words in the above text that are translated as filled. The first, which filled the dwelling, comes from the Greek *pleroo* which means: fill as a net with fish, a house with perfume; so as to complete or accomplish filling the atmosphere or a container. This Greek word speaks of filling the interior of a vessel, as the whole house.

The second, which filled the believers, comes from the Greek word *pletho*, a form of *pimplemi*. The word pletho means: to saturate and make fully wet, as by a soaking experience; to affect, influence, and have sway over as an inspiring stimulus; to supply, provide, equip, and make available for use. This Greek word speaks of absorption, a filling accomplished by an immersing engagement. A saturating fill is different than the mere filling of a vessel.

Our English word plethora is derived from the Greek *pletho*, and means: an excessive amount, overabundance. It speaks of overfill, much like what a sponge experiences when it is dipped; for a time the sponge oozes and drips with the soaking substance.

The solders at the crucifixion filled (pletho) a sponge and put it to the mouth of Jesus (John 19:29). The sponge was able to absorb, become saturated, and be ready for use.

Pletho was used several times in the book of Acts when

speaking of a fresh pouring upon, and a re-soaking of God's Holy Spirit: as with Peter (4:8), a group (4:31), an unrepentant Saul (9:17), and the anointed Paul (13:9).

Baptism in God's Spirit was then and now is a saturating, influencing, and equipping experience in the presence of God. Recipients of this spiritual experience are like sponges that absorb something of the presence of God they are experiencing. They are personally affected by the absorbed soaking and for a time, ooze and drip with the saturating influence.

Let me offer an example of how we absorb His presence. Have you ever used a natural sea sponge when you bathed? The property that makes them suitable for bathing is their ability to absorb water and cleansing agents. Their texture softens when placed in moisture, which enables them to be used on our skin but not be so tough as to scratch us. Technically, sponges are animals not plants. They feed by drawing nutrient rich water through their pores and filter cells. They seem vulnerable, yet sponges are very hardy and flexible. They can adapt their shape without harm.

Sponges are a useful metaphor for humans when it comes to discussing the presence of God in our lives. We can be solid and yet flexible. We can feed on all kinds of spiritual nutrients. The character, attitude, and personality (CAP) features of God, as found in Jesus, can be absorbed to become part of what and who we are becoming.

> *Jesus stood and cried out... "If anyone is thirsty, let him come to Me and drink. He who believes in Me...'From his innermost being will flow rivers of living water'"...this He spoke of the Spirit, whom those who believed in Him were to receive* (John 7:37-39).

Just as sponges absorb water, we can absorb the living water that Jesus spoke of—God's Holy Spirit. This absorbing feeds our spirit and has a lasting effect on how we go about living. This is why Scripture speaks of Holy Spirit as being poured forth, poured out, coming upon, and falling upon. Immersions are a result of the Spirit of God coming to and upon us, as absorbable recipients.

Our filling is a temporary soaking in the presence of God that allows us to absorb some of God's CAP. Like a sponge, to stay full enough to be dripping with God's influencing Spirit; we need to be refreshed often by His presence. These experiences of absorbing impartations become as a fellowship of our spirit with His Spirit.

Our filling is a temporary soaking in the presence of God that allows us to absorb some of God's CAP.

Soaking Spiritual Life

God has always sought to be our guiding light. His light is also spoken of as life-giving water. Remember, the baptism experience is not intended to be a one-time event. A one-time soaking does not bring lasting satisfaction nor does it create a joy that will not cease.

> Then He said to me... "I am...the beginning and the end. I will give to the one who thirsts from the spring of the water of life without cost" (Revelation 21:6).

> As the deer pants for the water brooks, so my soul pants for You, O God. My soul thirsts for God, for the living God (Psalm 42:1-2).

When we fail to respond to God's anointing and enlightening presence, we can lose our effectiveness as witnesses, which is why Scripture speaks of additional immersions.

> And now, Lord...grant that Your bond-servants may speak Your word with all confidence...And when they had prayed...they were all filled with the Holy Spirit and began to speak the word of God with boldness (Acts 4:29-31).

> And the disciples were continually filled with joy and with the Holy Spirit (Acts 13:52).

To better understand what happens in baptisms, we could relate the coming, going, and return of Jesus as a series of four transitions.

First, God's expressive voice entered the natural realm and transitioned into a human baby, to grow into manhood and visibly illustrate to the natural eye God's way of life.

Secondly, following his death, God raised the inactive body of Jesus into a state that could be seen, felt, and heard. In this transitional form, he was not always recognized.

Thirdly, as he ascended into the spiritual realm to once again function as God's spoken expression, Jesus left their natural sight and returned to function as the voice of God.

Fourthly, God comes to immerse people into the fellowship of His Spirit. In this function Jesus would invite us into an intimate interaction with God's presence.

To recap: 2000 years ago, God's voice, His spoken expression, entered flesh to live among men as a visible person, Jesus Christ. Now God's voice comes to us as God's Holy Spirit, to share with us empowering and maturing insights. While God has come in the past and will come in the future, we are to know Him in our present time:

> "I am the Alpha and the Omega," says the Lord God, "who is and who was and who is to come, the Almighty" (Revelation 1:8).

In essence, Jesus said, "I will come to you" as the Holy Spirit, to be "God with us." While God is one, He manifests and reveals himself to us in a variety of ways.

God does not require that we see or experience everything that was evident in the initial outpouring of His Spirit. Immersions in His presence can be brief moments that can happen anywhere and at any time. He knows, and you can know, if you are receiving any of His insights and absorbing the values of His character, attitude, and personality (CAP).

We can experience soaking immersions in God's presence in a variety of ways. It can be a graphic event when you lose some self-control. It can be the feel of a cleansing wash or the lifting of a burden. God's presence can bring a sense of refreshing, as though drinking from a water brook. We can sense Him revealing an insight regarding Scripture or concerning a situation in life. God's presence is not limited to any specific method, time, or place. We can be simply walking, jogging, driving, or while in a crowd, in conversation, or meditating in a quiet place.

Insightful encounters can happen anytime we are open and sensitive to His still small voice or gentle nudging. I once felt impressed to give a certain individual a sum of money. When the person received the check, they shared how they had been praying about a financial need. The amount of the check was exactly the amount of their need.

At times, an absorbing experience will have a permanent effect on us, however, we have to give ourselves to the transforming process of working out our issues. Our efforts, cooperating with God's refreshing presence, help establish the qualities of God's CAP in our own CAP.

> *My beloved…work out your salvation with fear* [reverential awe] *and trembling* (Philippians 2:12).

We can view Spirit baptisms as the Father and Jesus coming to us as Holy Spirit because each personality (Father, Son, and Holy Spirit) is an expression of the Eternal I Am. Spirit immersions invite us to interactively fellowship with God's presence in more intimate ways. Intimate fellowship is what helps us mature into His image and likeness more rapidly. We just need to be receptive to His provision.

> *Ask, and it will be given to you; seek, and you will find; knock, and it will be opened to you* (Matthew 7:8).

> *Blessed are those who hunger and thirst for righteousness, for they shall be satisfied* (Matthew 5:6).

> *The water that I will give him will become in him a well of water springing up to eternal life* (John 5:14).

God's presence dwells with each of us as an ever-present source of help through life. Additionally, we can partake of immersions in His presence where we, like a sponge, absorb insights and some of the character, attitude, and personality (CAP) traits of Jesus. It is in His presence that we find answers to our deepest questions.

When I hear someone say, "I received the baptism of the Holy Spirit at such and such a time," I congratulate them and ask, "Have you experienced immersions in His presence since then?"

Some people have expressed a caution concerning Holy Spirit immersions as though it were something weird or "spooky." Nothing could be further from the truth. Although the initial reactions of some people are rather dramatic, not everyone responds in the same way.

God's influencing presence makes us aware that He is more than an imagination. Immersions are invitations to receive from and respond to God's presence. As well as seeking an initial baptismal experience, I encourage you to pursue the continual interactive fellowship of God's presence.

When we look to God as our Father, like Jesus did (John 14:6), our experiences in His presence allow us to absorb more of our Father's CAP, much like a child who revels in the presence of a loving and adoring parent or grandparent.

We want to remember that every living person has a deposit of the Spirit of God residing in them, "the spirit of life." The deposit of God's Spirit in each of us is what causes us, even atheists, to cry out "Oh God!" when we encounter a catastrophe. Each time we interact and fellowship with God's presence, our spirit can absorb value from His Spirit.

Our spirit enables us to use each of our five senses to hear, feel, and see realities that exist beyond what our natural senses can perceive. Everyone can sense God's presence, receive eternal perceptions, go beyond sensing God's presence to interacting and having fellowship with God-in-Christ.

Again, an initial baptism is intended to introduce us to the fact that we can experience God beyond an initial cleansing event. We can interact with the Spirit presence of the Eternal One during this life. Our lifetime goal is to become more and more Christ-like, sons and daughters who spend time partaking of God's presence and becoming reflective resemblances of our Father.

Memorize: *As the deer pants for the water brooks, so my soul pants for You, O God. My soul thirsts for God, for the living God* (Psalm 42:1-2).

Questions for reflection:

1. What did the day of Pentecost celebrate?

2. We can be filled with Holy Spirit. What is meant by "filled"?

3. How does anyone grow and mature to be effective witnesses of Christ?

Chapter 8

Our Enlightening Guide

During my teenage years, my parents and I with two of my brothers traveled the country, visiting one ministry after another. We often drove straight through rather than stop for the night. On one occasion when I was 12 years old, we were driving through the deserts of Arizona late in the evening. A well-celebrated healing and deliverance evangelist of the day maintained his headquarters there. The weather was clear and peaceful as is common in the desert at night; the sky was a beautiful sight with a myriad of stars overhead.

All of a sudden we saw a big black bird fly straight into the front of our car. The lights on the car still worked so we kept driving. After a few minutes I began to feel sick and soon became nauseous. Sensing I was about to heave, I asked Dad to stop the car. He pulled over to the side of the road and I quickly got out.

I immediately threw up and lost consciousness. Dad said it

looked like someone picked me up and flipped me into the barbed wire fence along the side of the road, some ten feet away. As he jumped out of the car, Dad heard a voice say, "He is dead, go bury him."

My father quickly responded by racing over to me, grabbing my arm, and yelling "No!" while jerking me away from the fence. At that moment I regained consciousness and asked what had happened. As my parents cleaned me up and related the mystifying event, I began to feel normal again and we hit the road. Needless to say, I am very thankful Dad did not just accept what he had heard. If he had, I might still be next to that highway road but six feet under.

In today's world, multiple voices are crying out for us to listen. We want to learn to discern which ones are from God and which ones aren't. This experience taught me to be careful, as my dad was, for my life depended on it. The voice he heard was certainly not a voice from God for it was the voice of death.

Our Invitation

Our heavenly Father has always desired to fellowship with His offspring as He did with Adam and Eve. Before the coming of Jesus, God's presence was manifested and experienced in a variety of ways. He appeared as an angel, spoke as a voice, abided as a presence, and moved among them as the Holy Spirit. God miraculously intervened, healed infirmities, gave revelatory impressions, and was an influencing presence:

> *Then His people remembered the days of old, of Moses. Where is He who...put His Holy Spirit in the midst of them?* (Isaiah 63:11)

As for the promise which I made you when you came out of Egypt, My Spirit is abiding in your midst; do not fear! (Haggai 2:5)

Then he came to a cave...behold the word of the LORD came to him...And behold, a voice came to him and said... (1 Kings 19:9, 13).

For thus says the high and exalted One Who lives forever, whose name is Holy, "I dwell...with the contrite and lowly of spirit in order to revive the spirit of the lowly and to revive the heart of the contrite" (Isaiah 57:15).

But men moved by the Holy Spirit spoke from God... (2 Peter 1:21).

While there were many unrecorded occasions, Scripture records how God's presence communed daily with Adam and Eve, walked with Enoch, visited often with Abraham, became as a friend to Moses, spoke to the multitudes at Mount Sinai, and communicated through many who spoke as prophets. Peter said the voice people heard was the Holy Spirit. The Eternal I Am interacted with those who were receptive and responsive.

Jonah, who once ran from God's presence, despite his own desire for judgment, was taught to forgive. King David understood that his spirit needed the renewing, reviving, and stabilizing effects of God's presence. David expressed in a prayer his desire for God's renewing presence to remain with him:

Create in me a clean heart, O God, and renew a steadfast spirit in me...Do not cast me away from Your presence, and do not take Your Holy Spirit from me (Psalm 51:11).

The Eternal I Am came to people as a presence that was felt and not always seen. Many, who lived in the days when Jesus walked among us, experienced God's Holy Spirit. More often than not, people only knew God as the One who could, and on occasion, would intervene.

Moses asked to know God beyond the miracles—to know and understand His ways with mankind. David reports in the Psalms (103:7) that Moses did fellowship with God's presence and learned His ways. David was one of many who knew God as an anointing presence. A contemporary of David was the prophet Samuel who, also as a child, began to hear God and fellowship with His presence.

God has always desired to be our guiding influence through this life. The experience began with the first couple and has continued throughout history. He invites each of us into the fellowship of His presence.

Glorious Oneness

Two thousand years ago, when the times of the New Testament began, the expressive voice of God came to live among mankind as Jesus Christ. His ministry for three years was a visual illustration of "God with us." Scripture informs us that the logos—the voice of God, as Holy Spirit—caused Mary to conceive and bear a son, Jesus (John 1:14; Matthew 1:20). Thirty years later at his water baptism, God's Holy Spirit descended upon Jesus in a baptism experience, hovering as a dove (Luke 3:22).

In the life and ministry of Jesus, God illustrated to all observers that He desires to walk with us through life as an anointing and insightful presence. God wants to be more than the Fix-it-Guy we call on when in trouble. He desires to guide us through life, sharing His insight with us, and occasionally carrying us through our difficulties.

During his ministry on earth, the soul of Jesus (his mind, will, emotion) was one with his Father because he was in agreement with the Eternal I AM.

Between the 14th and 17th chapters of John, Jesus spoke much about his leaving so he could prepare a place for each of us in our heavenly Father's house. He was getting ready to leave the limitations of human life, so he could reveal more intently that we can experience an interactive fellowship with the presence of God during this life.

> *In My Father's house* [household] *are many dwelling places...I go to prepare a place for you...I will come again and receive you to Myself, that where I am, there you may be also* (John 14:2-3).

The level of fellowship we experience brings us into greater degrees of agreement with our heavenly Father.

Jesus spoke of the Father's household as dwelling places. Our dwelling in God's presence provides opportunity for degrees of intimacy. These abiding experiences refer to levels of fellowship and degrees of interaction with the presence of God.

The level of fellowship we experience brings us into greater degrees of agreement with our heavenly Father.

Where was Jesus when he said, "that where I am, there you may be also"? He was still living a physical life on the earth. As a human, Jesus was one with his Father by agreement. His fellowship with God kept him aware of what the Father was saying and doing. As a son, Jesus sought to say what he sensed God was saying and do as God led and directed him:

> *For I did not speak on My own initiative, but the Father Himself who sent Me has given Me a commandment as to what to say and what to speak* (John 12:49).
>
> *Jesus answered and was saying to them, "Truly, truly, I say to you, the Son can do nothing of Himself, unless it is something He sees the Father doing; for whatever the Father does, these things the Son also does in like manner"* (John 5:19).

The anointed man, Jesus, lived in intimate fellowship with his heavenly Father. As God's Spirit dwelled with His human son, so God's presence desires to dwell with us and provide many opportunities for us to interact with Him. Jesus spoke of this spiritual interaction as becoming one with our Father's loving heart and purpose.

Jesus then clarified how we, as he did, are to look to the Eternal I Am for guidance:

> *Pray... "Our Father who is in heaven, Hallowed be Your name. Your kingdom come. Your will be done, on earth as it is in heaven"* (Matthew 6:9-10).

"I say to you, if you ask the Father for anything in My name, He will give it to you" (John 16:23, 26).

Contrary to some perceptions, God is not a Spirit that possesses us. Growing and developing children need to learn to make good decisions. God wants to be the primary influence that leads, guides, and teaches us what His character, attitude and personality (CAP) looks and acts like.

Our Agreement

His exit from the natural life on earth enabled Jesus to once again function as the logos, God's expressive voice (clarified in chapter 5). As the voice of God, Jesus reveals and facilitates our spirit-to-Spirit fellowship with God. Jesus also, as the voice of God, interacts with the full body of Christ simultaneously, all around the globe.

The glory which You have given Me I have given to them, that they may be one, just as We are one; I in them and You in Me...Father, I desire that they...be with Me where I am (John 17:23-24).

Clearly, the glorious oneness Jesus spoke of was his agreement with the heart of God. So how do we agree with the heart of God and be one with the Father and one with His example son? Notice the bonding factor in this foundational declaration of Jesus:

And He said to him, "'You shall love the Lord your God with all your heart, and with all your soul, and with all your mind.' This is the great and foremost commandment. The second is like it, 'You shall love your neighbor as your-

self.' On these two commandments depend the whole Law and the Prophets" (Matthew 22:37-40).

The Law and the Prophets, in that day, was a phrase used to identify all Scripture. These two instructions are really one, with two supportive functions. Our love for God and our respectful love for one another are the foundational values that support everything God says to us and seeks to do through us. The life of Jesus demonstrated this concept of oneness.

After his life as the son of man, the spirit and soul of Jesus returned to again function as the expressive voice of God. Now, as the Holy Spirit, God invites us into the same interactive fellowship of His presence. God wants us to know Him as more than the one we call on in an emergency and as more than the one who came 2000 years ago.

Our dwelling in the Father's fellowship, as His household, is based first on our love, reverence, and appreciation of Him. Our fellowship with one another is also based on our ability to lovingly care and show concern for each other. These two expressions are tied together as one. Our love for God is not fully experienced without our becoming expressions of love to one another. God's loving attitude must flow into and through us before it can be fully established in us.

Francis Schaeffer writes about the importance of reaching beyond theological boundaries:

> It is in the midst of a difference that we have our golden opportunity. When everything is going well and we are all standing around in a nice little circle, there is not much to be seen by the world. But when

we come to the place where there is a real difference, and we exhibit uncompromised principles but at the same time observable love, then there is something that the world can see, something they can use to judge that these really are Christians, and that Jesus has indeed been sent by the Father." —*Complete Works Vol. 4*

Some people tend to want to qualify fellowship on the basis of what we believe, as though we must agree with each other's understanding before we can be in fellowship. One verse is commonly used to justify the idea: *Can two walk together, except they be agreed?* (KJV) This Old Testament verse in the original Hebrew does not really support the idea. The NASB is a more accurate translation:

Do two men walk together unless they have made an appointment? (Amos 3:3)

Amos said we must agree to walk together or we won't. In other words, our fellowship only works if we agree to walk together in spite of our differences. Think about it—do any two people believe alike on everything? Friendships, even marriage relationships, only work well if we agree to love each other, while respecting and appreciating the other's differences.

Jesus even had differing thoughts with God, as witnessed in his prayer, "If there is another way…" (Matthew 26:39).

Most of what we believe tends to change as we go through different stages of life. What we think and how we relate naturally differs in each stage—as a child, as a teenager, adult, spouse, or grandparent. Our growth from infancy into any level of maturity involves adjustments to what we believe to be true during each stage of growth. It can be very difficult to interact with an adult that still thinks and acts like a child.

Most of what we believe tends to change as we go through different stages of life.

Although our current season affects who we spend most of our time with—parents with young children versus those with older children, a balanced life involves some interaction with people in each stage of life. We want to remember that while everyone is different, in God's household love is the bonding factor—our love of God and of one another.

The love that originates with the Eternal I Am is patient, kind, hopeful, unfailing, faithful, and enduring. God's love is not envious, arrogant, selfish, provoked, inappropriate, or holds a grudge. The love of God should remain our motivator and shine through, even while we deal with each other's short-comings (1 Corinthians 13:4-8).

While Scripture references walking in the Light to experience fellowship, real fellowship is based on our love rather than the light we are able to perceive. Our ability to see and appreciate the enlightening insights shared by "the Light of Life" tends to improve as our love for God and our love for one another grows and develops.

Our Enlightening Guide

God is Light, and in Him there is no darkness at all...if we walk in the Light as He Himself is in the Light, we have fellowship with one another...If we say that we have no sin, we are deceiving ourselves and the truth is not in us (1 John 1:5-10).

No one "is" light; we all "walk in" the Light. The light we are able to see brings enlightenment and change to what we understand – our personal belief system. Our love however, if it is as God loves, remains a constant through our erroneous activity and our changing transformations.

Remember, sin is what we think and do independent of God. We all err, not only in what we do but in what we think and believe as well. God, however, looks beyond our errors and His love for us remains true. While light is a factor, love creates the strong foundation of God's household.

Our Father's household is a place of fellowship where we learn of Him. We become one with God only to the degree that we come into agreement with His heart's character, attitude, and personality (CAP). Our fellowship with one another is really based on "who" we believe rather than "what" we believe. It is in our fellowship with God that we see how His heart beats and we learn to be an appropriate influence on others.

Everyone is invited to actively dwell in glorious oneness with the Eternal I Am and know the same agreement Jesus demonstrated. When we know God as Jesus did, as obedient sons and daughters, we experience God as Father and are able to draw on His loving heart.

In his Sermon on the Mount, Jesus spoke to his followers about sharing their light as value that originates with God's light, when he said:

> *Let your light shine before men in such a way that they may see your good works and glorify your Father who is in heaven* (Matthew 5:16).

As we live and abide in the love and attitude of Jesus, we learn how to live more fully as disciplined children of God. As a parent, you want your children to become mature adults. In the same way, our heavenly Father wants us to "grow up in all aspects" into Him, who is the head, even Christ (Ephesians 4:15).

Interactive Members

The disciples accepted Jesus during the first coming as a physical presence to follow. During his transition from a physical presence to a spiritual presence, they began to realize he actually could always be with them as a presence of Spirit.

On that day of Pentecost the people received the anointing presence of Christ as a soaking immersion in God's Spirit. Immersions in Holy Spirit were then and are now, absorptions in God's Spirit that invite us into the experience of intimate fellowship with God-in-Christ as the enlightening voice of God.

The Gospel of Luke records what Jesus began to do and teach (Acts 1:1-2). Luke's book of Acts proceeds to record what Jesus continued to do and teach through the many membered body of followers. In other words, Jesus continued

Our Enlightening Guide

to do and teach but in a different way than before. Scripture calls those who partake of this fellowship, the body of Christ:

> ...*speaking the truth in love, we are to grow up in all aspects into Him who is the head, even Christ, from whom the whole body, being fitted and held together by what every joint supplies, according to the proper working of each...causes the growth of the body for the building up of itself in love* (Ephesians 4:15-16).

This gathering into the fellowship of faith became the new and ongoing visual of "God with us" on the earth. His loving presence is our bonding factor, creating his many-membered body. This fellowship of followers forms the body of Christ and is the visible witness of Christ that the world's natural eye can observe.

Isaiah proclaimed centuries before that this fellowship of believers was to be a reality:

> *"You are My witnesses," declares the LORD, "and My servant whom I have chosen, so that you may know and believe Me and understand that I am He...I am the LORD, and there is no savior besides Me. It is I who have declared and saved...so you are My witnesses," declares the LORD* (Isaiah 43:10-12).

The Eternal I Am declares He is our Savior. Jesus is the expressive voice of the I Am that came into human life as a man, to reveal God's forgiveness and His desire for fellowship with us as our loving Father. The above passage speaks of a plurality of witnesses in this life, who function as the body of Christ, as a visible of "God with us."

The return of Christ as our immerser in God's Spirit has a greater worldwide effect than Jesus had when he walked the earth as a man. This expression of God equips believers to be effective witnesses of the One who came in flesh, and of his subsequent appearing as the Holy Spirit. Jesus spoke of this greater effect as the works of a living and growing body of believers:

> *Truly, truly, I say to you, he who believes in Me, the works that I do, he will do also; and greater works than these…because I go to the Father* (John 14:12).

The immersing invitation into the fellowship of God's presence began to attract people by the droves. Three thousand people responded on that first day. As people gathered to the fellowship of God-in-Christ and with each other, life began to have more meaning.

Functioning as the voice of God, Jesus clearly reveals the secrets of God's heart and leads us into greater realizations of the expressive heart character, attitude, and personality (CAP) of God. Our fellowship with God's presence allows us to receive of His heart.

Most people go through life experiencing God's presence in everyday situations and circumstances. Many times His intervention is not very obvious, like when He provides health, safety, and prosperity. At times we are not even aware He has intervened on our behalf; at other times we have no doubt, as with close calls that threaten our life, miraculous healings, and unexpected provisions.

Plurality of "You"

Scripture teaches us that all mankind—every person—are natural and spiritual beings. We are all born with a deposit of God's Spirit (commonly called the spirit of life). This spirit in us came from God and returns to Him (Ecclesiastes 12:7). It is this deposit of God's Spirit in us that enables us to consciously be aware that God exists and enables our interaction with Him.

Ever since the outpouring of God's Spirit over two thousand years ago as an immersing, empowering, enlightening, and equipping presence, people have experienced interactive moments with the presence of God. Our frequent immersion in His presence infuses us with more of His values and seeks to produce in us the same character, attitude, and personality (CAP) of God that was demonstrated in Jesus.

Our loving communication and interaction with God and one another is what forms us into Christ's body. The body of Christ is the collection of believers that have a variety of supportive functions. This collective body is often spoken of in Scripture with the plural pronoun "you."

When Paul wrote his Epistles, he addressed groups of believers. While Paul wrote a few letters to individuals, like Timothy and Titus, his letters and comments were generally made to the collective bodies of believers. Here are a few examples: To the Colossians (1:27) ...*Christ in you, the hope of glory;* to the Romans (8:10) ...*the Spirit of Christ is in you*; and in the first letter to the Corinthians (3:16) *the Spirit of God dwells in you.* These verses do not intend to say or indicate that Christ is in me or you individually. These letters were written to groups and speak of Christ as God's presence in the midst of our collective function, our interaction as believers.

While God-in-Christ is the head of our individual lives, Scripture uses the word "you" in these phrases and verses in a collective sense, to address believers as groups. It is the anointing Christ that "dwells with us, in our midst, and among us" that is our hope of glory. Our hope of glory comes from and is found Christ and His presence among us, it is realized in "our" function as the collective body of Christ (Colossians 1:18). Notice the plural factors that define who "you" really speaks of in the following New Testament verses (we add a clarifying [bracket] a few times).

> *You are fellow citizens with the saints and are of God's household...and being fitted together, is growing into a holy temple in the Lord...you also are being built together into a dwelling of God in the Spirit* (Ephesians 2:19, 21-22).
>
> *Just as God said, "I will dwell in them and walk among them; and I will be their God, and they shall be My people...and I will be a father to you, and you* [people] *shall be sons and daughters to Me," says the Lord Almighty* (1 Corinthians 6:16, 18).
>
> *The Spirit of truth, whom the world cannot receive, because it does not see Him or know Him, but you know Him because He abides with you and will be in you* [your midst] (John 14:17)
>
> *The mystery which has been hidden from the past ages...but has now been manifested to His saints...which*

is Christ in you [among you], *the hope of glory* (Colossians 1:26-27).

If Christ is in you...He who raised Christ Jesus from the dead will also give life to your mortal bodies [gatherings] *through His Spirit who dwells in you* [your midst]. *So then, brethren, we...* (Romans 8:9-12).

I bow my knees before the Father, from whom every family...that He would grant you [your interaction] *...to be strengthened with power through His Spirit...that Christ may dwell in your hearts through faith* (Ephesians 3:14-17).

Jesus even addressed people as collective groups.

Little children...Greater is He who is in you [your midst] *than he who is in the world* (1 John 4:4).

I in them and You in Me, that they may be perfected in unity (John 17:23).

Our interaction and communication with God and one another is what forms us into the collective dwelling of God. Yes, we all have the spirit of life, and we absorb aspects of God's Spirit in immersion moments, however, our hope and expectation is not in any of us but is in God-in-Christ. the Eternal I Am dwells in our midst and among our togetherness. It is in our interactive functions that we are the Temple of the Lord.

Jesus was asked, "Who is greatest in the Kingdom?" (Matthew 18:1). At the end of Jesus' response to the question he clarified the issue with a statement that set aside the importance of me and you as individuals.

The Fellowship of His Presence

For where two or three have gathered together in My name, I am there in their midst (Matthew 18:20).

Jesus switched the focus from "who is" to "we are." God is the only I Am, everyone else, while on the earth, is valued as connective members of the body of Christ. When we converse as children of God, we interact and fellowship in the name of Jesus (his identifying CAP). In this fellowship we absorb more of the One who is in our midst, with, and among us.

The indication of Christ being in you or me, in some sense is correct because our spirit is being transformed into the likeness of Christ. Thus aspects of Christ's character, attitude, and personality become a part of who we are. However, when Scripture uses the word "you," more often than not, it is speaking of a plurality of believers as collective and interactive members.

Why is this important? The perception of "God in me" can create a "better than you" or an "I Am" attitude in believers. When we give all credit to God who is with us rather than in me, we have less chance of saying or indicating "I did it" or it was "my prayer." We are to guard against a "better than you" attitude about ourselves.

> *With humility of mind regard one another as more important than yourselves...Have this attitude in yourselves which was also in Christ Jesus, who...did not regard equality with God a thing to be grasped* (Philippians 2:3-6).

> *Be of the same mind toward one another; do not be haughty in mind, but associate with the lowly. Do not be wise in your own estimation* (Romans 12:16).

The scriptural concept of "you," in a very small way, is personal. As we are immersed in God's Spirit, our spirit is affected. Others can then see many aspects of God's CAP in our expressions and actions. However, individually we reflect as a mirror and resemble as a child the image and likeness of God, we progressively become what we are created to be—mature children of God, with all our individual variations and differences.

God's enlightening and empowering presence is in our midst—in our interaction with one another. Everyone is, in a sense, a habitation of the Spirit of God, but together "we" become more so.

> *You also are being built together into a dwelling of God in the Spirit* (Ephesians 2:22).

More Abundant Life

As our mind, will, and emotion are transformed by our fellowship with God's presence, we receive and absorb His values. This is how we learn to more appropriately reflect and resemble the character, attitude, and personality (CAP) of God that Jesus illustrated.

We are all equipped to sense and experience the presence of God in at least three ways:

1. We become aware of God as the Eternal Spirit that intervenes in life.

2. Our decision to respond to God as our Father enables our loving interaction as His children.

3. Our immersions in the fellowship of His presence facilitate our maturing growth.

When we pray the simple prayer, "Come into my heart, Lord Jesus," we invite the Spirit of God to interact with us and reform us into disciplined children whose expressions resemble the heart of God. Our acknowledgement, "Yes, God is real and I want Him involved in my life," opens us up to a conscious awareness of God's ability to lead and guide us into fuller realities.

Our individual and collective fellowship with the presence of God creates a visible evidence of God in our lives: 1) by resurrecting our spirit from its deathlike separation from His fellowship, 2) by reconciling our soul to God's way of thinking and feeling, 3) and at times, by restoring our physical health. These improving aspects of life enable our interactions and conversations to more appropriately reflect and resemble His heart.

The presence of God can come to us in our different areas of need. He may visit as our Creator; He can enticingly appeal to us as our Savior; and He may anoint us into an intimate fellowship with His presence. God comes to both His wandering offspring and to His responsive children, desiring to be with us, among us, and in our midst.

God comes to both His wandering offspring and to His responsive children, desiring to be with us, among us, and in our midst.

Our Enlightening Guide

We may think or speak of God as our resourceful Father, as our savior Jesus Christ, as a Holy Spirit presence, or as our overseeing Lord and King. Whichever way you see God, He comes to help us, to lead and guide us, to reveal to us, and to dwell with us. He desires to comfort, enlighten, and fellowship with us as His growing and maturing children.

At times, God's presence is obvious as we find things happening to and in us: a breeze may be felt; a fresh breath may come within; a warm and cozy feeling may be noticed; a physical healing happens; an emotional release is experienced; a psychological or heart wounding receives a healing salve; an encouraging thought occurs; an insight is received; an attitude changes; or a loving hug is felt. These experiences are the result of the Eternal I Am interacting, communicating, and seeking to have loving fellowship with us.

When Scripture speaks of our fellowship with God and with one another, many times it uses the collective terms: Children of God, Body of Christ, Temple of God, and Israel. Each of these terms identifies our response to His presence with us. When we interact with Father, we function as Children of God; when we interact and support one another, we function as the Body of Christ; when we are in an attitude of worship, we function as the Temple of God; when we, as members of one another, illustrate the ways of God, we function as Israel.

Together, we become brighter reflective lights and can more effectively draw others to God. As members of the body of Christ on the earth, we are commissioned to minister the love of God and reconcile others to the life of God in Christ (2 Corinthians 5:18-20).

God, who reconciled us to Himself through Christ and gave us the ministry of reconciliation, namely, that God was in Christ reconciling the world to Himself...He has committed to us the word of reconciliation. Therefore, we are ambassadors for Christ, as though God were making an appeal through us...be reconciled (2 Corinthians 5:18-20).

By continually responding to God as Jesus did, in agreement, we become one with the character, attitude, and personality (CAP) of the Eternal I AM. Our receptive response to His presence enables us to absorb more of His heart's love. These absorptions equip us to effectively walk in His ways, day by day. Our heavenly Father's guidance brings newness of heart and improves everything: who we are, what we say, where we go, and what we do.

Jesus revealed that our life, with all its ups and downs, is meant to include an intimate fellowship with our Father. Our fellowship with Him and with His body on the earth (one another) helps us learn to walk in the ways of God.

As we walk in the fellowship of His presence, our lives are progressively transformed. We grow in maturity, purity, and integrity. Our families experience more love, security, peace, provision, discipline (or order), and forgiveness. Our businesses thrive because of Christ-like leadership and direction, protection, and productivity. As we spark one another into fruitful interaction, we become attractive illustrations of God's love and draw others into the life improving culture of Christ. Our gatherings and fellowships are able to shine like a city on a hill.

Our Enlightening Guide

I encourage you to ask God for the desire and wisdom to change. Begin to adjust your behavior, even if the changes seem like small steps. God's saving grace and mercy will assist your efforts.

God is in us as a source of life, with us as a transforming presence, and in our midst to empower our fellowship with Him and with one another.

Memorize: *Speaking the truth in love, we are to grow up in all aspects into Him who is the head, even Christ, from whom the whole body, being fitted and held together by what every joint supplies, according to the proper working of each...causes the growth of the body for the building up of itself in love* (Ephesians 4:15-16).

Questions for reflection:

1. How did the voice of God interact with people in Old Testament days?

2. How was Jesus, as a son, one with his Father, the Eternal I Am?

3. Is our fellowship with God and with each other based on our light or love?

Chapter 9

Today's Reigning King

Like many today, I was taught Jesus would return to earth in the future, on a specific day, to an earthly location, as a physical person, in a glorified body. This teaching says Jesus will return to earth as a physically visible person to set up a literal kingdom and rule the natural earth from Jerusalem. The kingdom of God on the earth would "then" begin.

One evening with friends, we began to discuss the second coming, when all of a sudden it was like a light came on. A fresh thought filled us with wonder and amazement, and a variety of Scriptures began to flood our minds, adding validity to the inspiring thought. We began to question if we've been looking for a type of coming that is not God's intention, much like believers did when the Messiah came two thousand years ago.

Following that evening, I dove into Scripture to verify that the insights we were sensing were truly from God. I questioned, does God intend a futuristic second coming event? This anticipation is proclaimed so often, but is it biblically credible? I discovered we were reading into Scripture what we were led to believe. As I looked further, my research of historical writings revealed that our fresh insight was not new.

I found that a second coming, a visual return of Jesus was not a common belief before 1900 and only became a widely accepted idea since the mid-1900s. The futuristic coming of a naturally visible personage of Jesus is a relatively new idea and has only been a dominant emphasis in Christian teaching for less than one hundred years. How did this concept of a second coming event become such a central focus in Christian theology? Read on and discover how the idea developed.

A Revealing Reformation

In 1517, the Catholic priest and educator Martin Luther hung a document, known as the Ninety-five Theses, on the door of the Wittenberg Castle Church. He proclaimed, among other things, two Scriptural principles: 1) People are forgiven by our faithful response to God, not by paying indulgences (fees) to the religious organization. 2) Every believer is a priestly minister of God's grace. This was revolutionary in that day.

Once Luther posted his declarations, which were published and widely distributed, he began to openly teach the insights he was finding in Scripture. Luther proclaimed each of us can go directly to God for forgiveness and that every believer is a a priest in God's eyes. Within a few months, emboldened by Luther's actions, protests began to spring up all over Europe against many official teachings. The Reformation had officially begun.

Over the next few years the Pope issued many papal bulls (proclamations) against Luther and his new teachings, branding Luther a heretic and warning everyone to dismiss his damnable views of Scripture. When Luther was put on trial for treason against the official teachings, he refused to recant, proclaiming, "Unless I am convinced by Scripture and plain reason..."

When the Pope insisted that he alone possessed the authority to interpret Scripture and his voice was as the voice of God, Luther began to see something he previously overlooked. Then in 1520 Luther began to openly counter the papal bulls stating the papal system was actually antichrist. John Wycliffe in 1378 was the first reformer to publically declare the papal system was antichrist.

As a result of the doctrinal warfare between Luther and the Pope, several priests began searching for ways to combat the Protestant Reformers' devastating claim that the papal system itself was antichrist. Their elite class distinction and elevated status as official ministers, as the representatives of God, was being threatened.

In 1585, nearly seventy years after Luther's Ninety-five Theses was posted, Francisco Ribera, a Spanish Jesuit priest, published a 500-page commentary on the book of Revelation: *In Sacrum Beati Ioannis Apostoli, & Evangelistiae Apocalypsin Commentarij*. In his document, Ribera painted the picture of a futuristic Antichrist person who would rule the world before being destroyed by a futuristic coming of Jesus to rule and reign. What a novel idea! If antichrist was a person who was yet to come, it could not be the papal rule and its system of priestly overlords.

This document was the first time in written history that antichrist was identified as an individual person. The avowed objective of this fictitious theory was to combat the Reformers in the sixteenth century. The official religious system adopted this futuristic approach toward antichrist as their defense against the Reformers' claim. The notions of a future Antichrist person and a second coming event of Jesus were rejected by all Protestants for the next 300 plus years.

Antichrist Attitude

Please keep in mind that the following information and comments are not intended to undermine or subvert the importance of spiritual fathers and mothers or Christ-like advisors in our lives. We are all called into these roles. While many believers do not bother to function in these callings, some devote themselves to being a godly influence.

Scripture uses the word "antichrist" only in John's Epistles, five times in the first and once in the second. In these passages John speaks of antichrist not as a person but as a plurality: is coming and have appeared (2:18); denies that Jesus is the anointed one, denies the Father and Son (2:22); does not confess Jesus, is coming and is already in the world (4:3); and as many deceivers (2 John 7).

The Greek word *antichristos* is translated in the New

Testament as "antichrist." The Greek means: instead of, in the place of, as an equivalent.

In the Reformers' day, the Old English word "anti" may have carried the same meaning as the Greek word in Scripture. Today, the word "anti" is used almost exclusively to mean: against, in opposition. Our newer translations have maintained the same wording as the old versions although its English meaning has changed. The "instead of" meaning of anti is often missed and we think "against." Much of today's confusion regarding antichrist is supported by our twentieth century English.

The scriptural antichrist is an attitude resident in those who think or act as though they are "in the place of Christ" in someone's life. This attitude seeks to be a substitute mediator between God and man, as a go-between. They have an attitude that seeks, as anointed ones, to replace Christ as a spiritual guide.

It was several years after Christ returned at Pentecost as an anointing presence that John wrote his Epistles. He proclaimed many antichrists were already active among believers, trying to elevate their importance as spiritual mediators between believers and God. They were already complicating the Gospel message of one-on-one interaction with God-in-Christ.

Paul appears to speak of this attitude in his second letter to the Thessalonians (2:1-8) with the phrases: man of lawlessness, son of destruction, and wicked one who opposes and displays himself as being God. (The Greek parousia—meaning presence, as explained in chapter 6, is erroneously translated as coming.)

In the midst of the Thessalonian passage, Paul says this mystery, although restrained (v.7), was already working in their day. As people began to usurp the place of the Spirit of Christ in lives, they opposed the presence that had already come to anoint, dwell with, and be in our midst.

Ignassus, 75 years after Pentecost, promoted the world's way of government among believers, saying every city should have a central overseer, a bishop. He taught believers to "follow their bishop as Jesus followed the Father, respect elders as apostles, and bring honor to bishops as unto God."

The activity of the antichrist attitude was restrained in the day of the Apostles. When the Apostles and that first generation of believers passed from the scene of time, apparently the restraints were being removed. Leaders from various areas began to be appointed as official bishops over believers; to be overseers and meditators between God and believers.

As Bishops were appointed, they assumed responsibility as anointed ones. This helped create new class distinctions that became known as "clergy and laity," leaders and followers. This was not God's idea—it was man's effort to manage believers.

In 325 AD, the newly converted Roman Emperor Constantine called for the bishops to gather for the first Council of Nicaea. This and the councils that followed began a process of deciding official doctrines and which teachings would be accepted or rejected. It was a grueling time because the bishops believed a wide range of things, many which were customized by their local area. When the inspirational guide of Christ in our personal lives and gatherings is negated and replaced by official unadaptable doctrines, it further complicates our freedom to seek God for insight and direction for our different situations.

Then in 500 AD the religious officials exerted restricting control and outlawed the reading of Scripture in any language but Latin. They proceeded to collect and destroy all other copies. For the next 1000 years, only officials were allowed to view the writings of Scripture.

Believers were taught they could not possibly understand spiritual matters and needed the appointed mediators to define what it said and meant. This began to hide the knowledge that Christ was with them and reduced their tendency to seek or hear God on their own. It eventually produced a nearly total allegiance to the system of clergy and official religious leaders who were appointed to mediate matters of faith.

Biblical Priesthood

Luther began to expose the religious system of representation that elevated the Pope to replace Christ in people's lives as a system that embodies the deceiving attitude of antichrist. At the core of Luther's message was the phrase, "the priesthood of every believer," which referred to the scriptural description of believers as "a kingdom of priests" and "a holy priesthood."

> *If you will indeed obey My voice and keep My covenant, then you shall be My own possession among all the peoples...and you shall be to Me a kingdom of priests and a holy nation* (Exodus 19:5-6).

> *You also, as living stones, are being built up as a spiritual house for a holy priesthood, to offer up spiritual sacrifices acceptable to God through Jesus Christ* (1 Peter 2:5).

This call to be God's special people was initially given to the multitude of believers that came out of Egyptian slavery. Following the life of Jesus, it is repeated to followers of Christ. While this insight was lost during the Dark Ages, Luther began to proclaim it as a scriptural invitation for people to walk with God once again.

We highly recommend you watch the excellent movie Luther released in 2003. It illustrates what life was like in his day for believers and ministers. There were godly and ungodly ministers both within and outside of the official religious system.

Scripture places the privilege and responsibility of the priesthood on each believer. Priests are those who minister to the heart of God with adoring hearts and minister godly encouragement to the needs of others. The only God appointed mediator between us and God is Jesus, who is now experienced as the presence of Christ in our midst. We are all called to be priestly people.

The only God appointed mediator between us and God is Jesus, who is now experienced as the presence of Christ in our midst.

It was 1000 years after Scripture was removed from believers that the invention of the Guttenberg printing press (1455) began to make copies of Scripture available to the multitudes. The Scriptures once again began to enlighten and encourage individual believers.

Again, this is not an indictment against today's pastors and ministers, and their Godly function in our lives. There are many gifted leaders who are living examples of having a personal relationship with God while they instruct and complement our personal relationship with God and with each other.

One Mediator

A mediator is one who settles disputes as an intermediary between parties.

> *For there is one God, and one mediator also between God and men, the man Christ Jesus* (1 Timothy 2:5).

Christ, as our mediator, seeks to reconcile our consciousness (mind, will, and emotion) with the thinking, understanding, and feelings of God's heart. While every person can intercede for others, our intercession improves our hearts rather than changes the mind of God. This mediator function belongs to Christ Jesus alone, the invisible Spirit presence of God that is with us.

The Protestant Reformation came as a breath of fresh air for believers. The availability of Scripture added verification to the reformers' message. It brought a measure of release to the hearts and minds held captive by the religious system that encouraged ignorance and blind servitude to itself as the mediator between God and man. In truth, we all have access to God and can experience His refreshing, anointing, and insightful presence for ourselves.

> *There is one body* [of Christ] *and one Spirit…But to each one of us grace was given according to the measure of*

Christ's gift...And He gave some as apostles, and some as prophets, and some as evangelists, and some as pastors and teachers, for the equipping of the saints for the work of service, to the building up of the body of Christ (Ephesians 4:10-12).

Contrary to a common approach toward this Scripture, God graces each believer to function in one or more of these "gifts *of* the body" of Christ. These gifts are not only for special people but are to equip each believer to contribute and minister to other members of the body of Christ.

What I'm referring to is a tendency to look to people for a word of direction from God, as our mediator, when we should be seeking to hear God for ourselves. We are all called to function as priests. However, we should not act as though we are Christ. We are the body of Christ. Jesus is the head of the body. We are not to play God!

The concept of a mediator between God and man was first introduced in Scripture following the Exodus from Egyptian captivity. God spoke to the full gathering of over two million people, called Israel, and each person is reported to have heard His voice speak words, possibly the Ten Commandments. Moses recounted the event:

Remember the day you stood before the Lord your God at Horeb, when the Lord said to me, "Assemble the people to Me, that I may let them hear My words"...Then the Lord spoke to you from the midst of the fire; you heard the sound of words, but you saw no form—only a voice...You said..."we have heard His voice from the midst of the fire; we have seen today that God speaks with man" (Deuteronomy 4:10-12; 5:24).

> Then they said to Moses, "*Speak to us yourself and we will listen; but let not God speak to us*" (Exodus 20:19).

Unfortunately the people shrank from such interaction and appointed Moses to be a mediator between them and God, preferring to keep God at a distance. So it is today, the antichrist attitude is not just the result of leaders' assumptions; too often we prefer it and support its function, rather than asking God and listening for ourselves.

It was only after this refusal to personally interact that God told them to, "construct a sanctuary for Me, that I may dwell among them" (Exodus 25:8). Following their reluctance to interact with Him, God gave them a priestly system, a code of conduct, and a form of worship to mediate and encourage their interaction with Him.

Following their rebuff of His presence, God instructed them to build a place with emblems, appoint ministers, and utilize sacrifices. This visible representation was only until they were willing to accept His invisible presence among them. This system of worship was not intended to solidify their request for human mediation, but rather to encourage their acceptance of His presence in their midst.

> *The Law has become our tutor to lead us to Christ* (Galatians 3:24).

The Law, a priesthood class, and a specific place to meet with God were only intended until they would personally accept and interact with the presence of God. There were many throughout the Old Testament days that experienced this one-on-one interactive fellowship with God but the bulk of

His people did not. The Eternal I Am does not intend for us to communicate with Him through human mediators—this was man's idea.

Believers in the first three centuries after the resurrection of Jesus did not have specific places to gather and worship, appointed ministers, or sacrificial offerings. These tools of mediation were not needed because they entertained the presence of "God with us," among them, and in their midst. When they gathered, each one contributed as they were able:

> *What is the outcome then, brethren? When you assemble, each one has a psalm, has a teaching, has a revelation, has a tongue, has an interpretation. Let all things be done for edification* (1 Corinthians 14:26).

Divide and Dilute

In 1829, nearly 250 years after Ribera created his fictional approach to antichrist and a second coming event, a sixteen-year-old girl in Scotland named Margaret MacDonald had a vision that portrayed Jesus descending onto a mountain. The vision was drawn, printed, and circulated to illustrate a visible appearing of Jesus that all could see with the natural eye.

The next year, a Protestant church leader, John Nelson Darby, came across the vision and visited Margaret's home. Darby had already begun to question if believers were experiencing the kingdom of God because their lives seemed to lack the full rule and reign of Christ. Having a heart for the plight of Jewish people, he began to wonder, maybe Jesus could return to Mt. Zion as a visible Messiah to gather the Jewish people and set up a future natural type of kingdom.

It wasn't long before Darby began to preach these new ideas. He included Ribera's futuristic approach of an Antichrist person who would gain power before a second coming event. Darby introduced several new ideas and interpretations of Scripture. The following are a few of his ideas:

1. Separate Scripture into natural and spiritual applications to explain God's purposes on the earth, apart from believers, as a natural kingdom for the Jewish people.

2. Divide God's interaction with people into ages or dispensational time frames and list the kingdom age as a future time that is yet to come.

3. Promote a futuristic Antichrist person that would gain control of the world and signal the soon return of Jesus to set up a natural kingdom with the Jewish people.

4. Create a rapture event (an escape) for spiritual Israelites, so they would be spared the worldwide tribulation judgment God would bring on those who opposed God.

These ideas became the basis of thought for the doctrines of futurism and formed what is now called Dispensationalism. The dispensational theology starts with the concept that all history is divided into five ages. These time frames are used to define how God operates in any particular age and restricts how people are able to respond to God. Over the years the names of the Ages have changed. In the 21st century, they are known as: Pre-flood, Patriarch, Law, Grace, and Kingdom.

For example, from Moses until Christ, God supposedly governed His people according to Law; and since the time of Jesus, God governs us by Grace. This promotes the notion that people were not extended grace during the age of Law, and the Law has no bearing on us during the age of Grace. Additionally, the kingdom of God is not functioning on the earth but is reserved until a future Age. This nonsense tends to dilute God's purposes in our lives today as only spiritual, reserving the natural realizations for another Age.

The strangest and most deceptive idea promoted by dispensationalism is that Scripture should be segregated into spiritual and literal applications. Darby introduced the idea of two different Israel peoples and said the purposes of God are different for each. He began to declare the call to believers is only as a spiritual Israel. The other Israel carries a literal promise to the natural descendants of Abraham. This approach totally ignores the transfer of God's kingdom representation from Judaism to believers in Christ:

> *The chief priests and the elders of the people came to Him while He was teaching…"I say to you, the kingdom of God will be taken away from you and given to a people, producing the fruit of it"* (Matthew 21:23, 43).

The leaders of Judaism knew Jesus was speaking to them and their generation (Matthew 23:36; 24:34). The dispensational suppositions seek to make any application of the kingdom of God in today's world only spiritual, mystical, or metaphorical. This would mean the reign of Jesus in our lives does not really include our natural life. Scripture, however, makes it clear that the kingdom rule of God in people's lives came to earth with Jesus two thousand years ago.

Darby created another theory, saying the kingdom went away with Jesus, and we are waiting for him to return and overthrow the Antichrist in order to reign. This thinking keeps many believers complacent, expecting an against-God person to arise and take control. This mindset creates a hopeful expectation of a future liberator and makes believers hesitant to reject any overly controlling measures being pushed on us, as if our troubling time must come. These ideas distort God's efforts to improve each of our lives today.

This thinking keeps many believers complacent, expecting an against-God person to arise and take control.

This theory eventually morphed into the idea that Jesus will actually return twice: once to visibly snatch believers into heaven for a while (a rapture event), and then a second time to forcibly take the earth away from an antichrist.

Our lives are complicated when Scripture is divided into spiritual or physical perspectives, restrictive ages, and futuristic expectations. These ideas brought confusion to the Gospel message by delaying, deflecting, and diluting its full experience in our lives.

A Changing Future

I have a few books in my library, published before 1900, which offer a complete presentation of Christian theology. (In 1873 A Complete System of Theology by Samuel

Wakefield; in 1885 Outlines of Theology by Alexander Vinet; and in 1886 History of Interpretation by F. W. Farrar). None of these books mention dispensations, a second coming event, an Antichrist, a spiritual versus literal application of Scripture, nor any mention of two different Israelite callings. These theories were not part of Christian thought before the 20th century.

It took over 100 years, nearly three generations, for futurism to become an accepted view among believers. The teaching was rarely even considered before Charles T. Russell published his highly successful book, The Divine Plan of the Ages, in 1886. His definition of the ages predicted that in early 1900 the Age of Grace would end, Jesus would return, a Messianic Kingdom would be set up, and heathen governments would fall.

Russell's book became a huge success, selling nearly five million copies before its 1916 revision. Russell claimed in the new book that the previous publication of his theology failed to find success with theologians because he contrasted futurism with accepted theology. In his revision he simply presented the new view without argument.

Full acceptance of the dispensational notions came slowly as the first half of the 20th century unfolded. Two huge influencing factors besides Russell's publication were: Scofield's notes published in 1909 in a Bible, promoting the ideas, and World War I bringing an end to many European aristocratic governments.

Eventually seminaries began to teach futurism as a systematic explanation of Scripture. Ministers graduating from seminaries were taught this ideology, and they began to preach it in their churches. By the 1950s, nearly 365 years after Futurism was first introduced, most believers have accepted and proclaim the idea that an Antichrist person will take control and signal a visible return of Jesus.

We can look back and observe how several dispensational notions have changed over its evolution. Unfolding history created a need to adjust conclusions. We've seen the end of the age of Grace extended several times from the early 1900s. Many public figures through this century have been identified as the Antichrist, in efforts to signal Jesus was soon to come.

The birth of the Israeli nation in 1948 seemed to finalize a general acceptance. Its proponents would say, "See, the Jews are gathering!" The original theory stated the Jews would gather to the appearing Messiah; now they gather into a functioning nation before the coming. So it is with fiction. Because the fictional age and physical coming seems to never come, it is now just promoted as "any day now."

Another advocate, Hal Lindsey, promoted the ideas with his book, The Late Great Planet Earth, which sold more than 35 million copies in the 1970s. In 1995 a highly successful book series of fiction novels (*Left Behind*) put an exclamation point on the idea, offering a novelistic approach of the rapture. People do like a good story.

This "other gospel" seeks to make the kingdom of God like the governments of this world, who force submission. What a contradiction to Jesus' own words:

Jesus answered, "My kingdom is not of this world. If My kingdom were of this world [order], *then My servants would be fighting...My kingdom is not of this realm"* (John 18:36).

What is the truth? While His kingdom reign is not of this world, it is experienced in this world. A vast majority of believers experience, in degrees, the promise of Jesus' return to reign as a presence of Spirit. The presence of God-in-Christ has resulted in realistic levels of fulfillment in each life that responds to His anointing and enlightening presence.

Our Future Is Now

The Greek word for Gospel has only been found in two other ancient Greek writings. To the people in those days, the word Gospel meant "too good to be true." A common phrase among believers in the first three centuries that followed the life of Jesus was, "God is with us."

The Reformers recovered the insight that the presence of God in our lives progressively changes the quality of life of everyone, from the inside out. The reign of God begins in our willing acceptance, and then works out our salvation (Philippians 2:12) by renewing our mind, will, and emotion, to affect our natural life as well. Our response to the presence of God was, and is to be, a full-life experience.

On the one hand, Jesus has returned as the Spirit of Truth and desires to be the primary influence in our lives. On the other hand, He comes again, anew every day, to share eternal qualities and insights with all who will receive.

---◆---

He comes again, anew every day, to share eternal qualities and insights with all who will receive.

---◆---

Anticipation is good but when anticipation is kept in a future that seems to never come, hope fades. Eventually our heart gets sick and we begin to wonder if the Gospel is really true. Some even long to leave this life too quickly.

Hope deferred makes the heart sick, but desire fulfilled is a tree of life (Proverbs 13:12).

If our anticipation is fulfilled each day by partaking of God's fellowship, we receive infusions of the eternal qualities He shares. We become more than testimonies of eternal life, we become living examples of the eternal life we are receiving, while in this world.

Our receptive response to the Eternal I Am renews our soul into agreement with Him, changing how we reason (mind), adjusting our commitments (will), and reviving our feelings (emotion). Our receptive response to God renews our consciousness toward spiritual realities and leads us into more godly living. This is how our natural life experience improves.

It can be helpful to relate the coming, going, and return of Jesus as transitions. The voice of God came onto the earth from a spiritual existence, to be the natural life of Jesus Christ. Then the spirit and soul of Jesus returned to the previous spiritual existence as God's voice. Not limited by natural time and space, God-in-Christ returns to dwell in our midst as an insightful and anointing presence.

Our experiences in His presence make us better reflections and resemblances of His heart. Our personal interaction and conversations with God enable us to receive eternal qualities so our lives become more visible witnesses of our heavenly Father.

Memorize: *For there is one God, and one mediator also between God and men, the man Christ Jesus* (I Timothy 2:5).

Questions for reflection:

1. In Scripture, what does the word antichrist speak of?

2. When and who brought the concept of a mediator into our faith response?

3. What should we relegate to a future?

Chapter 10

Our Developing Reality

As I mentioned in chapter nine, several years ago while I was enjoying an evening with friends, our conversation turned toward Scripture and the things of God. Before long, our discussion was on the second coming of Jesus.

A question was raised: If Jesus returned to earth as a person that was visible to the natural eye, wouldn't everyone focus on where he was and what he was doing or what he might do next? We all agreed. Everyone, believers and sceptics alike, would turn their attention toward the visible presence.

Then the question was asked: Would such a physical time and space personage begin to undo what God has tried to teach us about His presence with us and in our midst?

God is Spirit. His presence has always been with us, and His enticing voice has always sought to speak to us as a guiding influence. Would God really want us to look to a time and space type of personage and lose our developing dependence on His Spirit's anointing and enlightening presence?

God has gone to great lengths to invite us into an active spirit-to-Spirit fellowship with His presence, without a specific physical activity or manifestation. Our relationship with God has always been by faith as we consciously call on Him. Faith is a spiritual activity that is not dependent on any natural or physical evidence. Our faith is tied to and established through our ongoing experiences with His presence.

A paradigm shift began to occur as our understanding of the return of Jesus began to adjust. Let's look at some of the insightful passages in Scripture that, over time, helped to bring clarity to our questions.

His Kingdom Reign

In Old Testament days, King Nebuchadnezzar had a dream that disturbed him, but he could not remember what it was. God revealed to Daniel in a vision that the king's dream was given by God and depicted a new type of kingdom coming in the future:

> *You continued looking until a stone was cut out without hands...and it...became a great mountain and filled the whole earth...And in the days of those kings the God of heaven will set up a kingdom which will never be destroyed...it will itself endure forever* (Daniel 2:34-35, 44).

Most scholars agree Nebuchadnezzar's dream about the great statue represented the historically successive kingdoms of Babylon, Medio-Persia, Greece, and Rome. While the text does not say what this stone was cut from, it clearly came into existence without hands. This means its creation was a God thing, a heavenly activity. This stone kingdom would not be the work of man. God would bring this new reality into a different type of kingdom on the earth.

Several years later, under a different king, Daniel saw in another vision "one like a son of man" receiving a dominion that would not cease or pass away. This vision confirmed the previous vision. This new kingdom reality, among people of all nations, would last for all future time.

> *And behold...One like a Son of Man was coming, and He came up to the Ancient of Days...to Him was given dominion, glory and a kingdom, that all the peoples, nations and men of every language might serve Him. His dominion is an everlasting dominion which will not pass away...the saints of the Highest One will receive the kingdom and possess the kingdom forever, for all ages to come* (Daniel 7:13-14, 18).

God also spoke of this new reality to the Prophet Jeremiah and then repeats it through the Apostle Paul. This new kingdom would be made up of His people of faith and would be ratified by a new covenant. It would be written on their hearts as enduring values.

> *"Behold, days are coming," declares the Lord, "when I will make a new covenant with the house of Israel and with the house of Judah, not like the covenant which I made with their fathers in the day I took them by the hand to bring them out of the land of Egypt, My covenant which they broke...I will put My law within them and on their heart I*

Our Developing Reality

will write it; and I will be their God, and they shall be My people" (Jeremiah 33:31, 33; Hebrews 10:16).

This son of man came 400 plus years after Jeremiah's proclamation. The foretold coming one was Jesus Christ. The followers of this anointed one would experience this new kingdom reality for all future time. Believers in God-in-Christ became recipients of this new covenant. Their gathering to Christ would be as shining lights to the world. This is what God desired with old Israel, but they continually broke covenant with Him and their light failed to shine brightly.

During his ministry, Jesus spoke of this New Covenant and described many aspects of the kingdom of God, explaining how it was first and foremost a willing acceptance of God's governing influence. God's reigning influence in our lives is not like earthly kingdoms; it does not come by outward dominance and forceful subjection but rather is a matter of willful choice. This kingdom reign in peoples' lives comes from the heavens of eternity.

God's reign becomes part of everyday life by changing how we think, feel, and understand.

As we submit to the insightful guidance of His presence, the kingdom reign of God becomes our reality. It starts in our soul consciousness and becomes heart expressions. God's reign becomes part of everyday life by changing how we think, feel, and understand. These changes affect the quality efforts we put into what we do, where we go, and what we say.

Consider how the following New Testament descriptions of the Kingdom of God are so different from the world's way of thinking and have nothing to do with an earthly location or a time frame:

> *My kingdom is not of this world...not of this realm* (John 18:36).
>
> *Your kingdom come...will be done, on earth as it is in heaven* (Matthew 6:10).
>
> *The kingdom of God is not coming with signs to be observed...for behold, the kingdom of God is in your midst* (Luke 17:20-21).
>
> *Seek first His kingdom and His righteousness* (Matthew 6:33).
>
> *He rescued us from the domain of darkness, and transferred us to the kingdom of His beloved Son* (Colossians 1:13-14).
>
> *The kingdom of God is not eating and drinking, but righteousness and peace and joy in the Holy Spirit* (Romans 14:17).

In these verses, and there are many more, we see several important aspects of life in the kingdom of God. We see that although it is in our midst while we are "in" this world, it is not "of" this world. Why? The kingdom of God involves our interaction with the presence of God and with each other. As

God shares with us insights and characteristics of eternal life, we experience a reality that brings us out of darkness and into joy, peace, and righteousness.

This kingdom reign of God cannot be shaken and remains constant for all who partake. The rule and reign of God is relational. It is not relegated by law nor is it demanding. God invites us into this relational life and encourages us to grow and mature in its way of living.

In his Sermon on the Mount, Jesus identified nine conditions of blessing in God's kingdom. These are called the Beatitudes (Matthew 5:3-11). The first beatitude sets the stage for the rest with the phrase "for theirs is the kingdom of heaven."

Think about the identifying marks of His kingdom: those who are poor in spirit, who mourn, are humble and meek, hunger for righteousness, are merciful, pure in heart, are peacemakers, and even persecuted for righteousness. The kingdom of God is laced with all types of people with totally different criteria for citizenship.

Biblical "Last Days"

From the days of Moses, the people who respond to the reign of God in their lives have been called Israel. The Old Testament governmental system of judges, elders, priests, and kings eventually developed into the religious system of Judaism. The Jews in that day believed an anointed person would come to deliver them from oppression and set up a kingdom where they would rule as Daniel and Jeremiah prophesied.

Their Messiah did come but most missed out on the realization because he was not what they expected. When the leaders of Judaism refused Jesus and his approach toward a life filled with loving grace, Jesus announced the kingdom of God would be taken from their oversight and no longer be administered from the Temple or the city of Jerusalem.

> *"Therefore I say to you, the kingdom of God will be taken away from you and given to a people, producing the fruit of it"…the chief priests and the Pharisees…understood that He was speaking about them* (Matthew 21:43, 45).

The Jewish rulers listening to Jesus were warned that several judgmental woes would come to end their restrictive oversight and kingdom representation (Matthew 23:1-36). Here is the first woe:

> *But woe to you, scribes and Pharisees, hypocrites, because you shut off the kingdom of heaven from people; for you do not enter in yourselves, nor do you allow those who are entering to go in* (v. 13).

A woeful judgment was also coming upon the religious centers: Temple and Jerusalem.

> *Jerusalem, Jerusalem, who kills the prophets and stones those who are sent to her! How often I wanted to gather your children together, the way a hen gathers her chicks under her wings, and you were unwilling. Behold, your house is being left to you desolate* (Matthew 23:37-38).

> *Jesus came out from the temple and was going away when His disciples came up to point out the temple buildings to Him. And He said to them, "Do you not see all these things? Truly I say to you, not one stone here will be left*

upon another, which will not be torn down" (Matthew 24:1-2).

Jesus made it clear; the generation living in that day would experience these "end times" and "last days" judgments (Matthew 23:36; 24:34). The biblical last days that Jesus spoke of were not for our day, they were coming upon the Jewish system of oversight. The relevancy of its systems had come to an end.

The Jewish oversight of God's people was experiencing its last days. God's kingdom representation was about to be taken from the restricting Jewish perceptions and given to those who would actually produce the loving fruitful results of God's presence among them. People would again be drawn into God's purpose for life, as illustrated by the new Israel, the body of Christ.

The writings of the Jewish historian Josephus, a Jew who was educated by the Romans, describe the events in and around Jerusalem in 70 AD. After a siege, Jerusalem fell to a Roman army under Titus. The prophesied, unheard of horrors, were experienced as destruction came to Judaism's capital city and center of religion, the Temple. Here is a small excerpt of Josephus' description of the dire famine that ensued:

> Now of those that perished by famine in the city, the number was prodigious, and the miseries they underwent were unspeakable; for if so much as the shadow of any kind of food did anywhere appear, a war was commenced presently; and the dearest friends fell a-fighting one with another about it, snatching from each other the most miserable supports of life...But

why should I describe the shameless impudence that the famine brought on men in their eating inanimate things, while I am going to relate matter of fact, the like to which no history relates, either among the Greeks or Barbarians! It is horrible to speak of it, and incredible when heard. —*The History of the Destruction of Jerusalem* by Flavius Josephus, Book VI, Chapter III, Section 3

Peter's comments on the day of Pentecost, in Acts 2, said the prophet Joel announced "these last days." Paul went on to instruct people for all succeeding generations, to repent, receive, and become faithful to the fellowship of God's presence. Three thousand people responded and experienced God's presence upon and among them that very day.

The last days and end times Jesus spoke of in Matthew 21-24 came in 70 AD. The designation of Israel, from that time forward, belonged to followers of Christ. The forty years between the start of the ministry of Jesus in 30 AD and the destruction of Jerusalem in 70 AD witnessed a visible transfer of God's kingdom representation.

A People of Faith

God did not create a new religion but a new clarity of faith. Faithfulness to the purposes of God includes hearing Him speak and our obedience.

God's influencing reign becomes visible in our natural lives to the degree that we commit our heart and lives to becoming more Christ-like. As we respond to the presence of God, our mind (reasoning), will (belief system), and emotion (feelings) are able to adjust and make improving changes. The activation of our faith affects our natural experience, and we become living witnesses of the life of Christ.

It is those who are of faith who are sons of Abraham...So then those who are of faith are blessed with Abraham, the believer (Galatians 3:7, 9).

Israel was never a result of natural lineage even though heritage was important to them. Abraham's faith initially affected his family, but faith was never restricted to his physical lineage. Even today, the Jewish faith does not restrict any race from embracing Judaism.

After Abraham and his son Isaac passed from the scene of time, Abraham's grandson Jacob moved the family to Egypt where Jacob's son Joseph was seated next to the ruling Pharaoh. The family that came to Egypt was a combination of Jacob's eleven other sons and their families along with all their servants, an accumulation of 70 people (Genesis 46:27). Two generations after Joseph, a pharaoh came into power that enslaved Jacob's family.

It was in the next generation, the third generation after Joseph (Exodus 6:16-20), that God called Moses to lead His people out of slavery. The family of faith had multiplied as they were joined by a vast array of others who were enslaved by affliction and bondage.

The people that came out of Egypt were a mixed multitude of 600,000 men of war (Exodus 12:37-38). If we multiply the men by four, assuming a wife and two children (a small amount for that day), we see they numbered over 2-1/4 million people. This vast multitude was only three generations from Joseph and the original 70 who had entered Egypt! The people God called "Israel" were many more than the physical descendants of Abraham.

There are three passages in Scripture that identify the time of captivity as 400 and 430 years (Exodus 12:40; Acts 7:2-7; Galatians 3:16-17). When we consider the time factor began when Abraham entered Canaan, as the Galatians text says, it is easier to understand. The Exodus happened in the seventh generation from Abraham.

Everyone who was oppressed found the promises to Abraham were better than the life they were living. The call to be God's people Israel was inclusive of all who would gather to faith in the God of Abraham, the Eternal I Am.

There is another point that illustrates God's call to Israel was not based on natural linage. When God told Israel to not marry others, He identified "others" as the inhabitants of Canaan. Scripture also attaches a reason for this restriction: It was because the inhabitants of Canaan were so set in their ungodly ways that they would turn Israel away from faith:

> *You shall not intermarry with them; you shall not give our daughters to their sons, nor shall you take their daughters for your sons. For they will turn your sons away from following Me to serve other gods* (Deuteronomy 7:3-4).

Intermarrying with people who are devoutly committed to opposing the God of Israel was forbidden because they could complicate devotion to the Eternal I Am and turn hearts away from faith. After their deliverance from Egypt, God clarified the call to be His people had only two conditions, and both are elements of faith. Anyone and everyone can be members of His special people if they obey His voice and keep covenant:

> *If you will indeed obey My voice and keep My covenant, then you shall be My own possession among all the peoples, for all the earth is Mine; and you shall be to Me a kingdom of priests and a holy nation* (Exodus 19:5-6).

The above call to be God's people Israel was a repetition of what God said as they left Egypt. Anyone would be considered an Israelite if they believed in Abraham's God and became part of the community of faith. Their faith just needed to become a life commitment:

> *But if a stranger sojourns with you, and celebrates the Passover to the Lord, let all his males be circumcised, and then let him come near to celebrate it; and he shall be like a native of the land* (Exodus 12: 48).

God's call to be His people includes all people, nations and languages. This inclusiveness has continued all through history, regardless of natural lineage. The same call to faith is repeated to all who respond to God and act on their faith.

> *Be sure that it is those who are of faith who are sons of Abraham* (Galatians 3:7).

> *But you are a chosen people, a royal priesthood, a holy nation, God's special possession, that you may declare the praises of him who called you out of darkness into his wonderful light* (1 Peter 2:9).

Throughout human history the person of faith believes in the

Eternal I Am. People of faith experience God as a presence that abides in our midst and interacts with us as the Spirit of Truth. Paul verified this:

> *For we...put no confidence in the flesh...and count them* [physical pedigrees] *but rubbish so that I may gain Christ...the righteousness which comes from God on the basis of faith* (Philippians 3:3, 7-9).

The call to be "the Israel of God" begins as a faith response to God. Our faith response is followed by a commitment of soul (mind, will, and emotion). Our commitment, ideally, is to the degree that it affects our heart expressions and every aspect of our natural life as well. This call and life experience extends to "whosoever will" out of every tribe, nation, people, and to every generation. The Eternal I Am is very inclusive:

> *We have fixed our hope on the living God, who is the Savior of all men, especially of believers* (1 Timothy 4:10).

His Rule Among Us

Consider the obvious. Jesus declared that he and the Spirit of his Father were as one, in agreement (John 14:9-10). Before leaving this earthly life, Jesus declared he, as God-in-Christ, would never leave nor forsake his followers (Hebrews 13:5-6).

With the exception of two "little whiles" (his death and his ascension), he would be with believers forever (Matthew 28:20). As God's Spirit, Jesus would arise in our midst (Matthew 18:20); teach us (John 14:26); guide us (John 16:13-14); anoint us (1 John 3:27); and dwell with us (John 14:23).

The disciples accepted the anointed Jesus Christ during his ministry on earth, as a natural, visible presence to follow. Then the disciples received Christ as God's anointing presence. The return of the "Spirit of the Father and His son" as Holy Spirit is to invite us into the fellowship of the Eternal I Am and to enable us to become effective witnesses of God's anointing presence.

The physical coming of Christ, as the anointed One, was to reveal God's forgiving nature and to illustrate His image and likeness as a human. The return of Christ as a Spirit is to immerse us in God's Spirit—the presence of God-in-Christ.

We all agree that Jesus did not physically return on the day of Pentecost two thousand years ago. Do we really need to see with natural eyes before we believe Christ has returned to be with us? We can know, experience, and partake of the returned Christ as a Spirit presence in our lives today!

The first several generations of believers experienced the realization of Jesus' words recorded in Matthew and John, where He said: "I'm going away but I will be right back, I'll never leave you, I'll always be with you, every day, through it all, even unto the end" (John 14:27-28; 16:7, 16-22; Matthew 28:20).

We can know, experience, and partake of the returned Christ as a Spirit presence in our lives today!

You may ask, "To what end?" Actually many ends: the end of Jewish oversight of His kingdom people; the end of many personal times of trouble; the end of our earthly life; even the end of time (if there is such a thing). Jesus abides with us forever, as the Spirit of Truth who immerses us into a fellowship with God's presence.

Our interactive fellowship with Christ and with one another continues to establish his kingdom rule and reign in our hearts, one life and family at a time, community by community, and generation after generation.

Perceptions of the kingdom of God and the way King Jesus was to reign changed in those early days. As people submitted to the authority of God-in-Christ, they found deliverance from what troubled their hearts and minds. They sensed the presence of God deliver them from the situations of their day. Sometimes deliverance was from the situation, but sometimes deliverance came within the situation, bringing a restful peace and an overcoming attitude that kept them from succumbing to their circumstances.

> *Therefore we do not lose heart, but though our outer man is decaying, yet our inner man is being renewed day by day. For momentary, light affliction is producing for us an eternal weight of glory far beyond all comparison, while we look not at the things which are seen, but at the things which are not seen; for the things which are seen are temporal, but the things which are not seen are eternal* (2 Corinthians 4:16-18).

Our spiritual senses enable us to hear, see, and feel spiritual activity and sense what God is saying and doing. While we are in the midst of this world's troubles and its passing times, we can be at rest and have peace through the turmoil.

Consider the parable of an old man and his son. They were both avid lovers of horses and took great joy in riding together. One day, the gate to the stable was left open and the old man's prize stallion escaped. The townspeople tried to console him, but the old man said, "Do not worry, this may yet turn out for good."

Sure enough, a week later the stallion returned with a rare white mare. The old man was happy for this blessing. Later the father was riding his prize stallion and his son was riding the rare mare. In a freak accident, the mare stumbled and fell on the son's leg, breaking it. From that day on, the son would always walk with a severe limp.

Sometime later barbarians attacked the province where the father and son lived. The young men were drafted to repel the enemy. The son was not accepted for battle due to his physical condition. In the days that followed, many of the young men perished in battle, but the son was spared. Sometimes great blessings indeed come in disguise!

Jesus described the rule and reign of God in our hearts and lives as relational experiences. The Gospel (Good News) speaks of a relational Christianity. The fundamentals of this relational Christianity are defined in my book, *The Christ Culture*, where I describe the basic tenets of biblical faith as relational concepts. These foundational concepts are the relational "ways of God."

Each time we experience the presence of God-in-Christ, we

acquire more of God's heart character, attitude and personality (CAP). Our Christ-like love and interaction with one another enables us to more appropriately influence our families, communities, cities, nations, and eventually the whole world. As we gravitate into better functioning members of the body of Christ, the kingdom of God becomes more visible on the earth.

God draws us to himself with enticing invitations of a better life. His lordship is more like a loving and insightful Father. The Eternal I Am calls, beckons, leads, and guides each responder with a gentle patience. Since He created this earthly realm with its ups and downs, its ins and outs, He understands our plight and difficulties.

When we approach God as a child who revels in his Father's delightful presence, we can receive from Him and partake of His eternal qualities. We can learn to live as children of God who reflect and resemble His heart. As we become more Christ-like, each of our relationships improves because we relate to one another in more loving ways.

As we become more Christ-like, each of our relationships improves because we relate to one another in more loving ways.

The reign of God begins in spirit but it is not just spiritual; many times it includes a physical deliverance as well. The Apostle Paul experienced physical healing (blind eyes opened), physical protection (an asp bite that did not harm), physical deliverance (from death squads and prison), and miraculous supplies of needed physical provisions.

Yet, when Paul was taken prisoner and sent to Rome to dwell in prison for several years, God didn't deliver him from prison but kept him within it. God used the prison to teach Paul to be an overcomer and to be peaceful in whatever circumstances he found himself, whether he was experiencing plenty or was in need (Philippians 4:11). It was in the confinement of prison that Paul wrote most of the New Testament epistles, providing a written word for that generation and for the generations that followed.

Paul said that although the first generation of believers had known Christ according to the flesh, we will no longer know him that way. We are to see Christ through our spiritual eyes and know him through the activity of our spiritual senses. Our personal maturity helps us view each other no longer just according to flesh but through spiritual eyes as well.

Today, If You Will Hear

In Psalms 95:9-11 David referred to the delivered Israelites refusal to hear God's voice. In his letter to the Hebrews, Paul used the phrase David coined, to remind us of the importance of hearing the voice of God. For emphasis, Paul quoted it three times:

> *Christ was faithful as a Son over His house-whose house we are, if we hold fast our confidence and the boast of our hope firm until the end. Therefore, just as the Holy Spirit says, "Today if you hear His voice, do not harden your*

hearts"...encourage one another day after day..."Today if you hear His voice"...did not all those who came out of Egypt led by Moses...not enter His rest...because of unbelief..."Today if you hear His voice" (Hebrews 3:6-19; 4:7).

The people God delivered out of Egypt were unable to believe what He said because they did not really believe God spoke to people, even after hearing God speak to them. They preferred to keep a distance between them and the Eternal I Am. This also made it difficult for them to hear and believe what God communicated through Moses. It is true; secondhand information is not as good or effective as personally hearing for ourselves.

While God supplied Israel's needs during their 40 year wilderness journey, His people died without entering into the peace and rest He offered. We are encouraged to hear, believe, and accept God's direction so we can partake of the peaceful rest His insightful presence provides.

For we have become partakers of Christ, if we hold fast...For we who have believed enter into that rest...let us therefore be diligent to enter that rest (Hebrews 3:14; 4:3, 11).

It is in God's fellowship that we experience rest. If we are hearing God's voice, believing what He says, and we are obedient to His guidance, we can remain calm and have peaceful rest while living in this world of turmoil.

We can all hear the thoughts God shares with us. We can sense His leading and feel His nudging presence. We can

Our Developing Reality

sense God nudge us toward the right response; to go or stay, to say or not, to do or not.

> *He made from one man every nation of mankind to live on all the face of the earth, having determined...that they would seek God...and find Him, though He is not far from each one of us; for in Him we live and move and exist* (Acts 17:26-28).

The Eternal I Am is the real God of yesterday and is the God of tomorrow as well. However, what He is saying and doing today is more important to each of us than what He has said and done in the past or what He may say and do in the future. Remember, "Today, if you will hear His voice." Today is the balancing reality between yesterday and tomorrow for each of us.

> *If you will receive my words...make your ear attentive to wisdom, incline your heart to understanding; for if you cry for discernment, lift your voice for understanding...then you will discern...and discover the knowledge of God. For the LORD gives wisdom; from His mouth come knowledge and understanding* (Proverbs 2:1-6).

A close friend of mine shared with me his father's advice: "Forget not to communicate." We enlarge on this clarity to say: Forget not to communicate with God and with each other!

What did Jesus tell his disciples to teach? God's kingdom is at hand, right here, before you and in your midst! People are to respond and enter into the kingdom of God by interacting with His presence. The Spirit of the Father and son comes to us today as the Spirit of Truth, to fellowship with His adoring children. As our contrite heart fellowships with our heavenly Father, His kingdom comes in our midst as it is in heaven, unlimited by time and space.

The rule and reign of Jesus Christ has come. Are you negating its power and ability to give us life more abundantly because you don't really believe it?

Consider the following prayer:

> Lord, may this be the last days of our allegiance to a confusing and ineffective perception of You and Your will! May I respond to Your presence as the Spirit of the Father and son—the Holy Spirit of Truth; may I be more aware of the insightful fellowship of Your presence and grow into a mature child of God; may I receive Your enabling power and be a witness of Your marvelous forgiving favor; may I cease to look to another as a replacement for my one-on-one fellowship with You; may I become more personally responsive to Your influencing reign. Even so come, Lord Jesus, into my life and situation today, again and again and again.

Our Developing Reality

Memorize: *If you will indeed obey My voice and keep My covenant, then you shall be My own possession among all the peoples, for all the earth is Mine; and you shall be to Me a kingdom of priests and a holy nation* (Exodus 19:5-6).

Questions for reflection:

1. Is God's kingdom in the earth a spiritual or a natural reality?

2. How and when is God's kingdom realization to be experienced?

3. How well are we hearing and seeing what God is saying and doing today?

About the Author

Keith dedicated his life to our heavenly Father in his pre-teen years. During the teenage years, he became a strong student of the Scriptures. At 29 he married Nancy, and they have three children and five grandchildren.

Keith has ministered in a variety of churches, serving in many capacities including senior pastor.

For more than 20 years, Keith has helped authors with his warm, easygoing style in such publishing positions as Author/Editor Liaison, Director of Acquisitions, Assistant Publisher, and Literary Agent.

To contact Keith Carroll by email:
Keith@RelationalGospel.com

or write to:
Keith Carroll
PO Box 341
Newburg, PA 17240

Bi-Weekly Blog

Don't miss any of Keith's inspiring thoughts. In conjunction with his books, each blog focuses on insights that bring amazing clarity to Scripture, so we can more effectively apply eternal qualities to our daily lives. These encouraging posts are the ideal size for pondering, discussing, and helping you experience deeper intimacy with the presence of God—the Eternal One.

Sign up for his bi-weekly blog at http://relationalgospel.com

Who am I? Why am I here? These questions have been pondered down through the ages!

Created to Relate brings clarity and new insight into the design and function of the human body, soul, and spirit. Discover the clear difference between what you are as a being and who you are as a person. Light is shed on how we are designed to function and the difference between our soul and spirit. Keith's dissection of the human heart is ground-breaking. He unveils the mystery of life and how we live natural and spiritual lives, simultaneously.

You are invited to embark on an exciting journey through Scripture and discover God's creative intention for your life. Learn the truth about what it means to be made in the image and likeness of the Eternal One.

> "How we are designed to function and relate to God becomes clear, concise, and illuminating. This book is extremely helpful to all who want to walk in deeper intimacy with our creator." *–Catherine Zoller, Speaker and Author*

> "Whether you are familiar with Scripture and have some things figured out or you are a newcomer to the faith, hang on for a wonderful ride. Keith opens up not only Scripture, but a deeper understanding of the life processes we manage every day. This book is a sheer delight..."
> *–Sandi Querin, MBA, JD., Th.D, Pastor, Clovis, California*

Welcome to the culture of Christ: an environment filled with rich appreciation for the ways of God!

The *Christ Culture* is a fresh way of looking at God's desire for our life on earth. This culture is an environment where God's inspiring presence is experienced and Christ-like attitudes and behaviors are encouraged. Light is shed on the most important concepts of our faith walk. Learn what are the "Ways of God," what are the seven processes of salvation, and why things happen as they do. How do God's methods of living bring us into His heart's desire?

Come on a life improving journey and explore the maturing ways of God among us. As we connect the dots, you'll receive new clarity about life. You'll see how to best apply the ways of God to your personal life so you more correctly reflect and resemble God.

"I have reviewed countless manuscripts over the past 30 years, but found few have had this clarity." –*Don Nori Sr., founder, Destiny Publishers*

"I highly recommend this book to anyone looking for purpose and meaning in life. *The Christ Culture* is a roadmap that takes you on a remarkable journey that will leave you completely transformed." –*Mary E. Banks, MSN, SPHR, Author*

Can we actually hear God speak?
Is intimacy with the Eternal One possible today?

Yes, God invites each of us into *The Fellowship of His Presence!* The Eternal One is not just a distant super Being who spins galaxies from His fingertips. His Fatherly heart loves us more than we can comprehend. Keith shares insights to bring amazing clarity to the Gospel message and shows there is no reason to wait for a second coming of Jesus—He is already "with us" as a presence of Spirit.

The multi-faceted nature of God becomes clear. New light is shed on the tree of the knowledge of good and evil. You'll discover how a fiction became an accepted theology, the antichrist is not a person, and when the biblical "last days" actually occurred.

How do we mature into God's creative intention? Discover how we can interact with the Eternal One and live as Jesus did. Our intimacy with God improves everything.

"This book is written with an amazing depth and understanding. Throughout these pages, it is clear that keeping Jesus and our fellowship with him at the forefront of all our doctrines and ideals is the most important thing we can do." *–Sandra Querin, JD, MBA, Th.D., Pastor, The Revival Center, Clovis, CA*

Additional Resources

Please visit:
http://relationalgospel.com
where you can find:

Group Discussion Guides

Research has found that we retain 20% of what we hear, 50% of what we hear and see, 70% of what we discuss, and 90% of what we do. Our retention is greatly increased when insights are discussed. Friendly conversation helps enlarge everyone's understanding and can ease the application of new insights into our daily lives.

To facilitate group discussions, chapter by chapter, we have put together a leader's resource packet for each of our books. Our guide includes these helpful resources:

- Tips on how to engage conversation in small groups

- Hand-outs with 12 to 14 discussion questions for each chapter

- Before and after participant evaluation forms

Our guide is a must-have resource to make your group experience more effective.

Sizable discounts are available on orders of 6 or more copies of one title. As a bonus, we include, free of charge, this valuable guide as a professionally prepared pdf file.

www.ingramcontent.com/pod-product-compliance
Lightning Source LLC
Chambersburg PA
CBHW070059020526
44112CB00034B/1818